A Moveable Feast

Ernest Hemingway was born in Chicago in 1899, the second of six children. In 1917, he joined the *Kansas City Star* as a cub reporter. The following year, he volunteered as an ambulance driver on the Italian front, where he was badly wounded but decorated for his services. He returned to America in 1919, and married in 1921. In 1922, he reported on the Greco-Turkish war before resigning from journalism to devote himself to fiction. He settled in Paris, associating with other expatriates like Ezra Pound and Gertrude Stein. He was passionately involved with bullfighting, big-game hunting and deep-sea fishing. Recognition of his position in contemporary literature came in 1954 when he was awarded the Nobel Prize for Literature, following the publication of *The Old Man and the Sea*. He died in 1961.

Ernest Hemingway

A MOVEABLE FEAST

THE RESTORED EDITION

Foreword by Patrick Hemingway

Edited with an Introduction by Seán Hemingway

arrow books

Published by Arrow Books 2011

3 5 7 9 10 8 6 4

Copyright © 1964 by Ernest Hemingway Ltd.
Copyright renewed © 1992 by John H. Hemingway,
Patrick Hemingway and Gregory Hemingway
Restored edition copyright © 2009 by the Hemingway Copyright Owners
Foreword copyright © 2009 by Patrick Hemingway
Introduction copyright © 2009 by Seán Hemingway

First published in the United States in 2009 by Scribner, a division of
Simon & Schuster, Inc.

First published in Great Britain in 2010 by Jonathan Cape

Arrow Books
The Random House Group Limited
20 Vauxhall Bridge Road, London, SW1V 2SA

www.randomhouse.co.uk

Addresses for companies within The Random House Group Limited can be found
at: www.randomhouse.co.uk/offices.htm

The Random House Group Limited Reg. No. 954009

A CIP catalogue record for this book
is available from the British Library

ISBN 9780099557029

The Random House Group Limited supports The Forest Stewardship Council
(FSC®), the leading international forest certification organisation. Our books
carrying the FSC label are printed on FSC® certified paper. FSC is the only forest
certification scheme endorsed by the leading environmental organisations,
including Greenpeace. Our paper procurement policy can be found at
www.randomhouse.co.uk/environment

MIX
Paper from
responsible sources
FSC® C016897

Printed and bound by CPI Group (UK) Ltd, Croydon, CR0 4YY

Picture Credits
1, 2, and 9. Family Collection; 3. Collection of Man Ray; 4. Copyright Estate of
Sylvia Beach. From the Collection of Sylvia Beach, Paris; 5. Photograph by Gisèle
Freund, Paris; 6. From the Sylvia Beach Collection, State University of New York at
Buffalo; 7. Collection of Man Ray; 8. Courtesy of Mrs. Samuel J. Lanahan

CONTENTS

A MOVEABLE FEAST

THE RESTORED EDITION

FOREWORD

A new generation of Hemingway readers (one hopes there will never be a lost generation!) has the opportunity here to read a published text that is a less edited and more comprehensive version of the original manuscript material the author intended as a memoir of his young, formative years as a writer in Paris; one of his best moveable feasts.

From the very beginning, there have been different editions of important works of literature. Take the Bible, for example. When I was a young person being raised in the Roman Catholic religion of my maternal grandmother, Mary Downey, born in County Cork, I heard it read from the pulpit during sermons on Sundays and feast days, and I read it myself, the Douay-Rheims Version (DRV) of the Bible, which is not the King James Version (KJV) although the DRV is literally closer more often to the Latin Vulgate Version (LVV).

Consider just the two opening lines:

DRV:

1. In the beginning God created the heaven and the earth.
2. And the earth was without form, and void; and darkness was upon the face of the deep. And the Spirit of God moved upon the face of the waters.

KJV:

1. In the beginning God created heaven, and earth.
2. And the earth was void and empty, and darkness was upon the face of the deep; and the spirit of God moved over the waters.

LVV:

1. *in principia creavit deus caelum et terram.*
2. *terra autem erat inanis et vacua et tenebrae super faciem abyssi et spiritus dei ferebatur super aquas.*

After googling all three of these versions, I was left with the distinct impression that I had a choice, because of the ambiguity of the LVV, between the Spirit of God being carried along floating on the stream like a piece of Sargasso seaweed or, alternatively, soaring along just above it like an albatross on the southern seas.

To me, anyway, soaring seems more godlike, and evidently, the Protestant clergymen in charge of the KJV thought the same. Neither the Protestants nor the Catholics could turn to God for answers to such ambiguities, and such is the case with Hemingway. He died before he had decided on a preface, chapter headings, an ending, and a title for his memoir, and no one, just like the case with the old gaucho's mother in Hudson's *Far Away And Long Ago*, has been able to reach him so far regarding these matters.

Now what can I say about the title? Mary Hemingway derives it from a remark made by her husband to Aaron Hotchner: "If you are lucky enough to have lived in Paris as a young man, then wherever you go for the rest of your life, it stays with you, for Paris is a moveable feast."

When my father was free to marry my mother, Pauline, he agreed to convert to Roman Catholicism and undergo a course of religious instruction in Paris. Hemingway, of course, as a boy had received quite a bit of religious instruction as a properly brought-up Protestant, but he had received the sacrament of last rites from a Catholic chaplain in the battlefield dressing station during the night after his mortar wound on the Italian front, and like the famous French king whose statue he mentions in the Paris memoir, he knew that Pauline was worth a mass.

I imagine that the priest, most likely from Saint-Sulpice, the church where Pauline attended services near her Paris apartment, took his role as instructor very seriously. One of the concepts he must have discussed with my father was that of the moveable feast. He would have explained that these are important church feast days linked to the varying date of Easter, so that they also have varying dates. Hemingway must have remembered then one of the most memorable speeches of Shakespeare, the feast of St. Crispin speech, the Agincourt address to his troops by Henry V. St. Crispin's day is not a moveable feast. It is the same date in the calendar of every year, but if you fought there on that day, it becomes your moveable feast.

The complexity of a moveable feast lies in the calculation of the calendar date for Easter in a given year, from which it is simple enough then to assign a calendar date to each and every moveable feast for a given year. Palm Sunday is seven days before Easter.

The calculation of the calendar date for Easter is no simple matter. This calculation has a special name, the Computus. No less a mathematician than Carl Friedrich Gauss came up with an algorithm for the computation. How those two, instructor and pupil, must have enjoyed themselves with these arcane discussions. I wonder if James Joyce might have joined in!

In later life the idea of a moveable feast for Hemingway became something very much like what King Harry wanted St. Crispin's Feast Day to be for "we happy few": a memory or even a state of being that had become a part of you, a thing that you could have always with you, no matter where you went or how you lived forever after, that you could never lose. An experience first fixed in time and space or a condition like happiness or love could be afterward moved or carried with you wherever you went in space and time. Hemingway had many moveable feasts besides Paris: D-Day on a landing craft going in to Omaha Beach among many others. For this to work, however, you need memory. With memory gone, and knowing that it is gone, is likely to come despair, the sin against the Holy Ghost. Electric shock therapy can destroy memory like dementia or death does, but, unlike dementia or death, you are left aware that it has been destroyed.

Now that I have tried to prepare you for it, here is the last bit of professional writing by my father, the true foreword to *A Moveable Feast*: "This book contains material from the *remises* of my memory and of my heart. Even if the one has been tampered with and the other does not exist."

Patrick Hemingway

ACKNOWLEDGMENTS

First, I thank Patrick Hemingway for suggesting the idea of this book to me, entrusting me with the task, and also for his sterling collaboration. It has been a rare privilege to work directly with my grandfather's manuscripts. In its own way, this project has been a moveable feast that I have worked on in many different places over several years. I am most grateful to Michael Katakis, Literary Rights Manager of the Hemingway Foreign Rights Trust, and to Brant Rumble, my editor at Simon & Schuster. At the John F. Kennedy library in Boston, I want to acknowledge the unwavering support of Deborah Leff, the former director, and Tom Putnam, the director, as well as Susan Wrynn, the curator of the Hemingway Collection. Without their kind assistance, this project would not have been undertaken. I am also grateful to James Hill at the audiovisual archives of the Kennedy library for assistance with photographic images and to Peter Duffield for allowing the use of his photograph on the back cover.

The knowledge I have accumulated over the years about my grandfather and his work has come from many sources. For this project, I single out for thanks my parents, Valerie and Gregory Hemingway, as well as Patrick and Carol Hemingway, Jack Hemingway, and George Plimpton. I also thank Joseph and Patricia Czapski, Patrice Czapski, Liisa Kissel, and J. Alexander MacGillivray. In researching this project, I have consulted numerous scholarly studies and remembrances of Paris in the 1920s, some of which are cited in my introduction. In particular, the monograph-length studies of *A Moveable Feast* by Jacqueline Tavernier-Courbin and Gerry Brenner were most helpful and will remain fundamental references for any future studies of *A Moveable Feast*. Finally, I want to acknowledge my soul mate and raison d'être, Colette, who helped in many ways, and Anouk, who came along toward the end of this project, bringing with her understanding and joy.

Introduction

In November 1956, the management of the Ritz Hotel in Paris convinced Ernest Hemingway to repossess two small steamer trunks that he had stored there in March 1928.[1] The trunks contained forgotten remnants from his first years in Paris: pages of typed fiction, notebooks of material relating to *The Sun Also Rises*, books, newspaper clippings, and old clothes. To bring this precious cargo home to the Finca in Cuba on their transatlantic voyage aboard the *Ile de France*, Ernest and his wife Mary purchased a large Louis Vuitton steamer trunk. I recall as a child seeing that trunk in my godmother Mary's apartment in New York, and I can still remember its smart leather trim with brass fittings, pervasive Louis Vuitton logo, and the gold embossed initials, "EH." The trunk itself was easily big enough for me to fit into, and it filled me with wonder at the grand, adventurous life my grandfather led.

Hemingway may well have had earlier inklings of writing a memoir about his early years in Paris, such as during the long recuperation after his near-death plane crashes in Africa in 1954, but his reacquaintance with this material—a time capsule from that seminal period in his life—stirred him to action.[2] In the summer of 1957, he began work on "The Paris Sketches," as he called the book. He worked on it in Cuba, and in Ketchum, and even brought it with him to Spain in the summer of 1959, and to Paris in the fall that same year. By

November 1959, Hemingway had completed and delivered to Scribner's a draft of a manuscript that lacked only an introduction and the final chapter. *A Moveable Feast,* published posthumously in 1964, concerns the author's time in Paris from 1921 to 1926. Careful study of the manuscripts for *A Moveable Feast* reveals that relatively little material was reused from Hemingway's early papers and manuscripts.[3] Of particular note is the chapter on the poet Cheever Dunning, which can be directly linked to a very early draft of the story that Hemingway describes in a letter to Ezra Pound, dated October 15, 1924.[4] Additionally, parts of the chapter "Ford Madox Ford and the Devil's Disciple" were culled from material that Hemingway excised from *The Sun Also Rises* and had rediscovered in the notebooks he found in the trunks at the Ritz. While *A Moveable Feast* is the first and most complete posthumously published book by Ernest Hemingway, Mary Hemingway states, in her editor's note, that the book was finished in the spring of 1960, when he had completed another round of edits to the manuscript at the Finca. In actuality, the book was never finished in Hemingway's eyes.

This new special edition of *A Moveable Feast* celebrates my grandfather's classic memoir of his early days in Paris fifty years after he completed the first draft of the book. Presented here for the first time is Ernest Hemingway's original manuscript text as he had it at the time of his death in 1961. Although Hemingway had completed several drafts of the main text in prior years, he had not written an introduction or final chapter to his satisfaction, nor had he decided on a title. In fact, Hemingway continued to work on the book at least into April of 1961.

During the nearly three years between the author's death and the first publication of *A Moveable Feast* in the spring of

1964, significant changes were made to the manuscript by the editors, Mary Hemingway and Harry Brague of Scribner's. A small amount of material that Hemingway had intended to include was deleted, and other material that he had written for the book but had decided not to include, notably the chapter entitled "Birth of A New School," a large section of the chapter on Ezra Pound, now entitled "Ezra Pound and the Measuring Worm," and a large section of the final chapter, previously entitled "There is Never Any End to Paris" and now renamed "Winters in Schruns," was added. The introductory letter by Ernest Hemingway in *A Moveable Feast* was actually fabricated by Mary Hemingway from manuscript fragments and, thus, has been left out of this edition. Likewise, the editors changed the order of some of the chapters. Chapter 7 became chapter 3, and chapter 16 on Schruns was made into the last chapter with additional material added from a chapter in which Hemingway wrote about his break up with Hadley and new marriage to Pauline Pfeiffer, a text published in its entirety here for the first time as "The Pilot Fish and the Rich." Hemingway had decided against including this material in the book because he thought of his relationship with Pauline as a beginning, not an ending.

The nineteen chapters of *A Moveable Feast* published here are based on a typed manuscript with original notations in Hemingway's hand—the last draft of the last book that he ever worked on. The actual manuscript is in the Ernest Hemingway Collection at the John F. Kennedy library in Boston, Massachusetts, the primary repository for all of Hemingway's manuscripts.[5] Although this manuscript lacks a final chapter, I believe that it provides a truer representation of the book my grandfather intended to publish.

A number of relatively minor editorial changes were also

made to the published edition of *A Moveable Feast*, changes that I strongly doubt would have been attempted by the editor had she required the author's approval. These changes have been reinstated. The most significant of them, I think, is the changing in many places of Hemingway's use of the second person in the narrative, evident from the very first paragraph of chapter one and then throughout the book (see, e.g., Fig. 1). This intentional and carefully conceived narrative device gives the effect of the author speaking to himself and, subconsciously, through the repetition of the word "you," brings the reader into the story.

A particularly egregious edit was made to the foreword to chapter 17 on F. Scott Fitzgerald. Hemingway's final text (see Fig. 7) reads:

His talent was as natural as the pattern that was made by the dust on a butterfly's wings. At one time he understood it no more than the butterfly did and he did not know when it was brushed or marred. Later he became conscious of his damaged wings and of their construction and he learned to think. He was flying again and I was lucky to meet him just after a good time in his writing if not a good one in his life.

But in the posthumous edition, it reads:

His talent was as natural as the pattern that was made by the dust on a butterfly's wings. At one time he understood it no more than the butterfly did and he did not know when it was brushed or marred. Later he became conscious of his damaged wings and of their construction and he learned to think and could not fly any more because the love of flight was gone and he could only remember when it had been effortless.[6]

It is clear that the editors culled this text from an earlier draft (see Fig. 6) discarded by Hemingway, but this kind of editorial decision, which casts Fitzgerald in a less sympathetic light than Hemingway's final version, seems completely unwarranted.

Hemingway had only provided titles for three chapters of his original manuscript: "Ford Madox Ford and the Devil's Disciple," "Birth of a New School," and "The Man Who Was Marked for Death" (see Fig. 4). The titles from the first publication have been retained, except as noted above, for the clarity of the reader familiar with the book. Likewise, I have provided titles for the additional, previously unpublished sketches.

There was a great deal of material that Hemingway wrote for *A Moveable Feast* that he decided to leave out, acting "by the old rule that how good a book is should be judged by the man who writes it by the excellence of the material that he eliminates." At least ten additional chapters were composed for the book, each in varying stages of completion, and these have been included in this special edition as a separate section after the main text. None of these chapters were finished to the author's satisfaction and must be regarded as incomplete. Some of the chapters were written and rewritten in two drafts, and others are preserved in only a single handwritten first draft. As a corpus, I think that most readers will agree they provide a most interesting supplement to the book.

The chapters of *A Moveable Feast* do not follow a strict chronological order. Similarly, I have organized the additional chapters with a slightly idiosyncratic logic. "Birth of A New School" comes first because this chapter was already included in the first publication of the book, where the editors had placed it between "Ford Madox Ford and the Devil's Disciple" and "With Pascin at the Dôme." Hemingway wrote two different possible endings for this chapter, which were edited and partially conflated by the editors of A Moveable Feast. Both endings are provided here as Hemingway wrote them. Likewise, "Ezra Pound and His Bel Esprit" is material that was published in A Moveable Feast but had been written as a separate chapter, and, in fact, was cut by Hemingway.

"On Writing in the First Person" is next because it is quite different from all of the other pieces. It focuses on writing rather than a particular remembrance, and, as a piece about process, seems more appropriate at the beginning than at the end. While incomplete, it offers insight into the process of writing and pokes fun at the so-called "detective school" of literary criticism. Most young writers write fiction from their own experience but Hemingway, as he intimates in this brief sketch, culled a great deal of material from other firsthand and secondhand sources. For example, he writes about interviewing soldiers from World War I, and his mastery of historical fiction is never more evident than in his novel A Farewell to Arms, where he has recreated the retreat of Caporetto so accurately that one would not believe he had not been at the battle.[7]

"Secret Pleasures" is a story about Ernest wearing his hair long and deciding with Hadley to grow their hair to the same length. Most likely it is based primarily on the winter of 1922–23, when they were at Chamby sur Montreux, Switzerland, not Schruns, Austria, and is a case where Hemingway has altered the facts to improve the story.[8] The sketch, only preserved in a single handwritten draft, is audacious for its intimate portrayal of the author and his wife and recalls certain passages in Hemingway's posthumous novel, The Garden of Eden.[9] It gives a particularly vivid impression of Ernest Hemingway as a young professional with one good suit and one pair of dress shoes who needed to observe the social conventions and dress code of his job as a journalist. The length that one cuts one's hair remains a theme that resonates with young people today as they get their start in life. Hemingway conveys the complexity of motivations and assumptions in the simple act of growing his hair out: transitioning to his new bohemian lifestyle as a full-time writer of fiction, saving money both by not cutting his hair and not going out to the fashionable quarter because of his bohemian appearance, how this allowed him to focus on his writing, his journalist colleagues' disdainful impressions contrasted with the completely different cultural associations of long hair for Japanese men, whom Hemingway met at Ezra Pound's studio and whose long, straight black hair Hemingway admired. From this practical and anti-establishment act grows the idea that he and Hadley wear their hair at the same length as a kind of secret pleasure shared between them. Hemingway comically contrasts the scene in Paris with that in Schruns, where the local barber assumes that Hemingway is following the new Paris fashion and, consequently, encourages other customers to take up the style.

"A Strange Fight Club" is a story about a little-known Canadian boxer named Larry Gains and his irregular training at the Stade Anastasie, a dance hall restaurant in a tough part of Paris where fights were held as dinnertime entertainment and the fighters acted as waiters. It is an unusual portrait of Paris life in the 1920s and reveals the pugilistic side of Ernest Hemingway, who enjoyed boxing himself and often covered important fights as a journalist.[10] Hemingway, as when he spars with Ezra Pound in his studio, casts himself as the authority, which he displays to the reader through his careful assessment of Larry Gains's inexperienced moves.

"The Acrid Smell of Lies" is an unflattering portrait of Ford Madox Ford, whose breath was "fouler than the spout of any whale." Hemingway's intense dislike of Ford has long puzzled biographers, especially given Ford's often glowing praise in print of Hemingway's writing and the opportunities that Ford gave Hemingway as an assistant editor of *The Transatlantic Review*.[11] According to one theory, their falling out was the result of a dispute over money.[12] In this sketch, Hemingway ascribes his "unreasonable antipathy" toward Ford as his own inability to listen to Ford's constant lying.

"The Education of Mr. Bumby" is a sketch preserved in just one handwritten draft, in which Ernest and his son Jack, whose nickname was Bumby, join F. Scott Fitzgerald for a drink at a "neutral" cafe in Paris. The piece adds another example to Hemingway's portrayal of Fitzgerald's problems with drinking and his wife Zelda's jealousy over his writing. After telling Fitzgerald stories about World War I, Hemingway mentions to Bumby that their friend André Masson was damaged by the war but went on to lead a productive life as a painter. Masson served in the Great War for two and a half years until 1917, when he was wounded in the chest and suffered depression afterward. Masson shared with Joan Miró a Paris studio, which Hemingway visited on a number of occasions. Hemingway acquired three forest landscape paintings by Masson, all of which now hang in the Hemingway room at the John F. Kennedy library, and knowing that Masson was deeply affected by the war may explain something of their haunting effect.[13]

"Scott and His Parisian Chauffeur" is more a story about F. Scott Fitzgerald than about Paris—it takes place in America after a Princeton football game that the Fitzgeralds and Hemingways attended together in the fall of 1928. One can see why Hemingway decided to leave it out as it falls outside the general chronological parameters of the book. However, the black humor and automotive theme make the sketch a fine sequel to Ernest's earlier chapter on the drive with Fitzgerald from Lyon to Paris in his hoodless Renault, amplifying Hemingway's portrayal of "Scott's complicated tragedies, generosities and devotions."

To judge from the manuscripts (see, e.g., Fig. 5), the most difficult part of writing *A Moveable Feast* for Ernest Hemingway was coming to terms with his betrayal of Hadley with Pauline and the end of that first marriage. In a way this would have been a logical ending to the book, and one can see why Mary Hemingway decided on it for the ending. However, Hemingway, after writing a chapter about it, included in this edition as "The Pilot Fish and the Rich," decided that it was not the ending he wanted since he considered his marriage to Pauline a beginning, and this ending clearly left the heroine of the book, Hadley, abandoned and alone. What is worse is that only a part of "The Pilot Fish and the Rich" was incorporated into the last chapter of *A Moveable Feast* in the 1964 edition. The remorse that Hemingway expresses and the responsibility that he accepts for the breakup, as well as "the unbelievable happiness" that he had with Pauline, was cut out by the editors. For the first time, readers of this edition have the full text to consider as Hemingway wrote it. The extensive edits Mary Hemingway made to this text seem to have served her own personal relationship with the writer as his fourth and final wife, rather than the interests of the book or of the author, who comes across in the posthumous first edition as something of an unknowing victim, which he clearly was not (see also Fig. 5).

"*Nada y Pues Nada*" was written by Ernest Hemingway over three days, from April 1–3, 1961, as a possible final chapter for the book. It is the last demonstrable sustained piece of writing that Hemingway did for the book and is only preserved in a single handwritten manuscript (see Fig. 8). It is as much a reflection of the author's state of mind at that time, only three weeks before he attempted suicide, as it is a contribution to the book. His commitment to his work despite his failing health is remarkable, especially amid the paranoia and severe state of depression that he was facing. Writing, as he had done before in better times, that he was born to write "and had done and would do again" must have been difficult knowing that his writing was not going well and had not been for some time. In the final sentence, he writes that his memory has been tampered with, likely a reference to his recent visit to the Mayo clinic for shock therapy treatment, and that his heart no longer exists. As Hemingway's Spanish Civil War–time friend Antoine de Saint Exupery observed in his book, *Le Petit Prince,* it is only with the heart that we can see rightly, as the essence of things is not visible to the eye. Hemingway's expression of despair is a sad portent of the end for him, which came by his own hand less than three months later.

In a letter written to Charles Scribner, Jr., on April 18, 1961, but never mailed, Hemingway writes that he is unable to finish the book as he had hoped and suggests publishing it without a final chapter.[14] He mentions that he has been trying to write an ending for over a month. The false starts and endings included in the Fragments section of this volume probably belong to this time. He also provides a long list of tentative titles for *A Moveable Feast.* Hemingway had a habit of writing out lists of possible titles for his books from as early as his 1920s collection, *in our time.*[15] Some names were frivolous and some were serious, and he often liked to say that the Bible was the best source for finding titles.[16] At first glance, the list of titles Hemingway drew up at this time seems awful and may be an indication of how much his mind was deteriorating. They include: *The Part Nobody Knows, To Hope and Write Well (The Paris Stories), To Write It True, Good Nails Are Made of Iron, To Bite On the Nail, Some Things As They Were, Some People and The Places, How It Began, To Love and Write Well, It Is Different In The Ring,* and, my personal favorite, *How Different It Was When You Were There.*

The title that he tentatively settled on was *The Early Eye and The Ear (How Paris was in the early days).* This last title sounds a bit like a medical textbook that could have belonged to his father. In seriousness, though, I think that Hemingway was trying to get at what he believed were key facets of his writing technique with this title. The eye, a term usually used in the connoisseurship of fine art, draws an interesting comparison between writing and painting, a subject that Hemingway discusses in *A Moveable Feast,* especially his learning from the paintings of Cézanne.[17] Hemingway first developed his eye, his ability to discern the gold from the dross and turn his observations into prose, in Paris in the twenties. The ear, which we think of as more pertinent to musical composition, is clearly important to creative writing. Hemingway's writing typically reads well when spoken aloud. When complete, his writing is so tight that every word is integral, like notes in a musical composition. In his early years in Paris, he learned about the value of rhythm and repetition in writing from Gertrude Stein and, especially, James Joyce, whose masterpiece, *Ulysses,* published by Sylvia Beach at Shakespeare and Company, is an extraordinary virtuoso display of English prose that comes alive when read aloud.[18] *The Early Eye and The Ear* gets at the need to hone your craft, something Hemingway truly believed in and worked at all his life. It implies talent, for you must have a good eye and a good ear to begin with if you are to be successful, but it also suggests that you need experience to develop your abilities as a writer, and Paris at that time was for Ernest Hemingway the perfect place to do this. Indeed, many of the handwritten first-draft manuscripts of *A Moveable Feast* are extremely clean and serve as remarkable and poignant testimonies to Hemingway's talent (see Figs. 2–3), even in his final years. The deathless prose appears on the page fully formed like the goddess Athena born from the head of Zeus.

The final title of the book, *A Moveable Feast,* was chosen by Mary Hemingway after the author's death. It does not appear anywhere in the manuscript but was suggested to her by A.E. Hotchner, who recalls Ernest mentioning the phrase to him at the Ritz Bar in Paris in 1950.[19] The choice of spelling follows Hemingway's idiosyncratic preference to retain the "e" in words ending in "ing" and formed from verbs that ended in "e." It adds the imprint of the author, and the "ea" in *Moveable* also makes a pleasant visual repetition with the "ea" in *Feast*. In his foreword, Patrick Hemingway sheds light on the historical use of the term by my grandfather in his writing and at home.

Whether you are reading it for the first time or coming back to it like visiting with an old friend, *A Moveable Feast* retains a freshness that is remarkable. Recently, I was in Paris to bring a marble portrait bust of the Greek historian Herodotus from the Metropolitan Museum of Art to the Louvre for an exhibition on Babylon from the third millennium B.C. to the time of Alexander the Great and on into myth, when that great city became a place of legend and a biblical symbol of decadence. I was reminded of F. Scott Fitzgerald's fine short story, "Babylon Revisited," where he describes Paris as a place of excess, endless parties, and lurid decadence at the time that Hemingway first knew him in the mid-1920s, and how different Paris was for Fitzgerald at the end of the decade, during the Great Depression, when his own career was on a downward turn.[20] There were not many Americans in Paris during my recent visit, with the weak dollar and current economic difficulties at home. While for Hemingway in the 1920s "exchange was a beautiful thing," the pendulum has swung and American expatriate life in Paris is no longer cheap.[21] Paris was for me (and my grandfather rightly states each person's experience is different) an inspiring and vital place of beauty and light, and history and art.

For my grandfather, who was just starting out in those early years, Paris was simply the best place to work in the world, and it remained for him the city that he loved most. While you will not find goatherds piping their flocks through the streets of Paris anymore, if you visit the places on the Left Bank that Ernest Hemingway wrote about, or the Ritz Bar or Luxembourg Gardens, as I did with my wife recently, you can get a sense of how it must have been. You do not have to go to Paris to do this, though; simply read *A Moveable Feast,* and it will take you there.

Seán Hemingway

1

A Good Café
on the Place St.-Michel

Then there was the bad weather. It would come in one day when the fall was over. You would have to shut the windows in the night against the rain and the cold wind would strip the leaves from the trees in the Place Contrescarpe. The leaves lay sodden in the rain and the wind drove the rain against the big green autobus at the terminal and the Café des Amateurs was crowded and the windows misted over from the heat and the smoke inside. It was a sad, evilly run café where the drunkards of the quarter crowded together and I kept away from it because of the smell of dirty bodies and the sour smell of drunkenness. The men and women who frequented the Amateurs stayed drunk all of the time or all of the time they could afford it; mostly on wine which they bought by the half-liter or liter. Many strangely named apéritifs were advertised, but few people could afford them except as a foundation to build their wine drunks on. The women drunkards were called *poivrottes* which meant female rummies.

The Café des Amateurs was the cesspool of the rue Mouffetard, that wonderful narrow crowded market street which led into the Place Contrescarpe. The squat toilets of the old apartment houses, one by the side of the stairs on each floor with two cleated cement shoe-shaped elevations on each side of the aperture so a *locataire* would not slip, emptied into cesspools which were emptied by pumping into horse-drawn tank wagons at night. In the summer time, with all windows open, you would hear the pumping and the odor was very strong. The tank wagons were painted brown and saffron color and in the moonlight when they worked the rue Cardinal Lemoine their wheeled, horse-drawn cylinders looked like Braque paintings. No one emptied the Café des Amateurs though, and its yellowed poster stating the terms and penalties of the law against public drunkenness was as flyblown and disregarded as its clients were constant and ill-smelling.

All of the sadness of the city came suddenly with the first cold rains of winter, and there were no more tops to the high white houses as you walked but only the wet blackness of the street and the closed doors of the small shops, the herb sellers, the stationery and the newspaper shops, the midwife—second class—and the hotel where Verlaine had died where you had a room on the top floor where you worked.

It was either six or eight flights up to the top floor and it was very cold and I knew how much it would cost for a bundle of small twigs, three wire-wrapped packets of short, half-pencil length pieces of split pine to catch fire from the twigs, and then the bundle of half-lengths of hard wood that I must buy to make a fire that would warm the room. So I went to the far side of the street to look up at the roof in the rain and see if any chimneys were going, and how the smoke blew. There was no smoke and I thought about how the chimney would be cold and might not draw and of the room possibly filling with smoke, and the fuel wasted, and the money gone with it, and I walked on in the rain. I walked down past the Lycée Henri Quatre and the ancient church of St.-Étienne-du-Mont and the windswept Place du Panthéon and cut in for shelter to the right and finally came out on the lee side of the Boulevard St.-Michel and worked on down it past the Cluny and the Boulevard St.-Germain until I came to a good café that I knew on the Place St.-Michel.

It was a pleasant café, warm and clean and friendly, and I hung up my old waterproof on the coat rack to dry and put my worn and weathered felt hat on the rack above the bench and ordered a *café au lait*. The waiter brought it and I took out a notebook from the pocket of the coat and a pencil and started to write. I was writing about up in Michigan and since it was a wild, cold, blowing day it was that sort of day in the story. I had already seen the end of fall come through boyhood, youth and young manhood, and in one place you could write about it better than in another. That was called transplanting yourself, I thought, and it could be as necessary with people as with other sorts of growing things. But in the story the boys were drinking and this made me thirsty and I ordered a rum St. James. This tasted wonderful on the cold day and I kept on writing, feeling very well and feeling the good Martinique rum warm me all through my body and my spirit.

A girl came in the café and sat by herself at a table near the window. She was very pretty with a face fresh as a newly minted coin if they minted coins in smooth flesh with rain-freshened skin, and her hair black as a crow's wing and cut sharply and diagonally across her cheek.

I looked at her and she disturbed me and made me very excited. I wished I could put her in the story, or anywhere, but she had placed herself so she could watch the street and the entry and I knew she was waiting for someone. So I went on writing.

The story was writing itself and I was having a hard time keeping up with it. I ordered another rum St. James and I watched the girl whenever I looked up, or when I sharpened the pencil with a pencil sharpener with the shavings curling into the saucer under my drink.

I've seen you, beauty, and you belong to me now, whoever you are waiting for and if I never see you again, I thought. You belong to me and all Paris belongs to me and I belong to this notebook and this pencil.

Then I went back to writing and I entered far into the story and was lost in it. I was writing it now and it was not writing itself and I did not look up nor know anything about the time nor think where I was nor order any more rum St. James. I was tired of rum St. James without thinking about it. Then the story was finished and I was very tired. I read the last paragraph and then I looked up and looked for the girl and she had gone. I hope she's gone with a good man, I thought. But I felt sad.

I closed up the story in the notebook and put it in my inside pocket and I asked the waiter for a dozen *portugaises* and a half-carafe of the dry white wine they had there. After writing a story I was always empty and both sad and happy, as though I had made love, and I was sure this was a very good story although I would not know truly how good until I read it over the next day.

As I ate the oysters with their strong taste of the sea and their faint metallic taste that the cold white wine washed away, leaving only the sea taste and the succulent texture, and as I drank their cold liquid from each shell and washed it down with the crisp taste of wine, I lost the empty feeling and began to be happy and to make plans.

Now that the bad weather had come, we could leave Paris for a while for a place where this rain would be snow coming down through the pines and covering the road and the high hillsides and at an altitude where we would hear it creak as we walked home at night. Below Les Avants there was a chalet where the pension was wonderful and where we would be together and have our books and at night be warm in bed together with the windows open and the stars bright. That was where we could go.

I would give up the room in the hotel where I wrote and there was only the rent of 74 rue Cardinal Lemoine which was nominal. I had written journalism for Toronto and the checks for that were due. I could write that anywhere under any circumstances and we had money to make the trip.

Maybe away from Paris I could write about Paris as in Paris I could write about Michigan. I did not know it was too early for that because I did not know Paris well enough. But that was how it worked out eventually. Anyway we would go if my wife wanted to, and I finished the oysters and the wine and paid my score in the café and made it the shortest way back up the Montagne Ste. Geneviève through the rain, that was now only local weather and not something that changed your life, to the flat at the top of the hill.

"I think it would be wonderful, Tatie," my wife said. She had a lovely modeled face and her eyes and her smile lighted up at decisions as though they were rich presents. "When should we leave?"

"Whenever you want."

"Oh, I want to right away. Didn't you know?"

"Maybe it will be fine and clear when we come back. It can be very fine when it is clear and cold."

"I'm sure it will be," she said. "Weren't you good to think of going, too."

them and roasted chestnuts when I was hungry. I was always hungry with the walking and the cold and the working. Up in the room I had a bottle of kirsch that we had brought back from the mountains and I took a drink of kirsch when I would get toward the end of a story or toward the end of the day's work. When I was through working for the day I put the notebook, or the paper, away in the drawer of the table and put any *mandarines* that were left in my pocket. They would freeze if they were left in the room at night.

It was wonderful to walk down the long flights of stairs knowing that I'd had good luck working. I always worked until I had something done and I always stopped when I knew what was going to happen next. That way I could be sure of going on the next day. But sometimes when I was starting a new story and I could not get it going, I would sit in front of the fire and squeeze the peel of the little oranges into the edge of the flame and watch the sputter of blue that they made. I would stand and look out over the roofs of Paris and think, "Do not worry. You have always written before and you will write now. All you have to do is write one true sentence. Write the truest sentence that you know." So finally I would write one true sentence, and then go on from there. It was easy then because there was always one true sentence that you knew or had seen or had heard someone say. If I started to write elaborately, or like someone introducing or presenting something, I found that I could cut that scrollwork or ornament out and throw it away and start with the first true simple declarative sentence I had written. Up in that room I decided that I would write one story about each thing that I knew about. I was trying to do this all the time I was writing, and it was good and severe discipline.

It was in that room too that I learned not to think about anything that I was writing from the time I stopped writing until I started again the next day. That way my subconscious would be working on it and at the same time I would be listening to other people and noticing everything, I hoped; learning, I hoped; and I would read so that I would not think about my work and make myself impotent to do it. Going down the stairs when you had worked well, and that needed luck as well as discipline, was a wonderful feeling and I was free then to walk anywhere in Paris.

If I walked down by different streets to the Jardin du Luxembourg in the afternoon I could walk through the gardens and then go to the Musée du Luxembourg where the great paintings were that have now mostly been transferred to the Louvre and the Jeu de Paume. I went there nearly every day for the Cézannes and to see the Manets and the Monets and the other Impressionists that I had first come to know about in the Art Institute at Chicago. I was learning something from the painting of Cézanne that made writing simple true sentences far from enough to make the stories have the dimensions that I was trying to put in them. I was learning very much from him but I was not articulate enough to explain it to anyone. Besides it was a secret. But if the light was gone in the Luxembourg I would walk up through the gardens and stop in at the studio apartment where Gertrude Stein lived at 27 rue de Fleurus.

My wife and I had called on Miss Stein, and she and the friend who lived with her had been very cordial and friendly and we had loved the big studio with the great paintings. It was like one of the best rooms in the finest museum except there was a big fireplace and it was warm and comfortable and they gave you good things to eat and tea and natural distilled liqueurs made from purple plums, yellow plums or wild raspberries. These were fragrant, colorless alcohols served from cut-glass carafes in small glasses and whether they were *quetsche, mirabelle* or *framboise* they all tasted like the fruits they came from, converted into a controlled fire on your tongue that warmed you and loosened your tongue.

Miss Stein was very big but not tall and was heavily built like a peasant woman. She had beautiful eyes and a strong German-Jewish face that also could have been Friulano and she reminded me of a northern Italian peasant woman with her clothes, her mobile face and her lovely, thick, alive immigrant hair which she wore put up in the same way she had probably worn it in college. She talked all the time and at first it was about people and places.

Her companion had a very pleasant voice, was small, very dark, with her hair cut like Joan of Arc in the Boutet de Monvel illustrations and had a very hooked nose. She was working on a piece of needlepoint when we first met them and she worked on this and saw to the food and drink and talked to my wife. She made one conversation and listened to two and often interrupted the one she was not making. Afterwards she explained to me that she always talked to the wives. The wives, my wife and I felt, were tolerated. But we liked Miss Stein and her friend, although the friend was frightening, and the paintings and the cakes and the *eau-de-vie* were truly wonderful. They seemed to like us too and treated us as though we were very good, well-mannered and promising children and I felt that they forgave us for being in love and being married—time would fix that—and when my wife invited them to tea, they accepted.

When they came to our flat they seemed to like us even more; but perhaps that was because the place was so small and we were much closer together. Miss Stein sat on the bed that was on the floor and asked to see the stories I had written and she said that she liked some of them except one called "Up in Michigan."

"It's good," she said. "That's not the question at all. But it is *inaccrochable*. That means it is like a picture that a painter paints and then he cannot hang it when he has a show and nobody will buy it because they cannot hang it either."

"But what if it is not dirty but it is only that you are trying to use words that people would actually use? That are the only words that can make the story come true and that you must use them? You have to use them."

"But you don't get the point at all," she said. "You mustn't write anything that is *inaccrochable*. There is no point in it. It's wrong and it's silly."

"I see," I said. I did not agree at all but it was a point of view and I did not believe in arguing with my elders. I would much rather hear them talk and many of the things that Gertrude said were very intelligent. She told me that sooner or later I must give up journalism and I could not have agreed with her more. She herself wanted to be published in the *Atlantic Monthly,* she told me, and she would be. She told me that I was not a good enough writer to be published there or in *The Saturday Evening Post* but that I might be some new sort of writer in my own way but the first thing to remember was not to write stories that were *inaccrochable*. I did not argue about this nor try to explain again what I was trying to do about conversation. That was my own business and it was much more interesting to listen. That afternoon, too, she told us how to buy pictures.

"You can either buy clothes or buy pictures," she said. "It's that simple. No one who is not very rich can do both. Pay no attention to your clothes and no attention at all to the mode, and buy your clothes for comfort and durability, and you will have the clothes and money to buy pictures."

"But if I never bought any more clothing ever," I said, "I wouldn't have enough to buy the Picassos that I want."

"No. He's out of your range. You have to buy the people of your own age—of your own military service group. You'll know them. You'll meet them around the quarter. There are always good new serious painters. But it's not you buying clothes so much. It's your wife always. It's women's clothes that are expensive."

I saw my wife trying not to look at the strange, steerage clothes that Miss Stein wore and she was successful. When they left we were still popular, I thought, and we were asked to come again to 27 rue de Fleurus.

It was later on that I was asked to come to the studio any time after five in the winter time. I had met Miss Stein in the Luxembourg. I cannot remember whether she was walking her dog or not, nor whether she had a dog then. I know that I was walking myself, since we could not afford a dog nor even a cat then, and the only cats I knew were in the cafés or small restaurants or the great cats that I admired in concierges' windows. Later I often met Miss Stein with her dog in the Luxembourg gardens; but I think this time was before she had one.

But I accepted her invitation, dog or no dog, and had taken to stopping in at the studio, and she always gave me the natural *eau-de-vie*, insisting on my refilling my glass, and I looked at the pictures and we talked. The pictures were wonderful and the talk was very good. She talked, mostly, and she told me about modern pictures and about painters—more about them as people than as painters—and she talked about her work. She showed me the many volumes of manuscript that she had written and that her companion typed each day. Writing every day made her happy, but as I got to know her better I found that for her to keep happy it was necessary for this steady daily output, which varied with her energy, but was regular, and therefore became huge, to be published and that she receive official recognition.

This had not become an acute situation when I first knew her, since she had published three stories that were intelligible to anyone. One of these stories, "Melanctha," was very good and good samples of her experimental writing had been published in book form and had been well praised by critics who had met her or known her. She had such a personality that when she wished to win anyone over to her side she could not be resisted, and critics who met her and saw her pictures took writing of hers that they could not understand on trust because of their enthusiasm for her as a person, and their confidence in her judgment. She had also discovered many things about rhythms and the uses of words in repetition that were valid and valuable and she talked well about them.

But for her to continue to write each day without the drudgery of revision nor the obligation to make her writing intelligible and continue to have the true happiness of creation, it was beginning to become necessary for her to have publication and official acceptance, especially for the unbelievably long book called *The Making of Americans*.

This book began magnificently, went on very well for a long way with stretches of great brilliance and then went on endlessly in repetitions that a more conscientious and less lazy writer would have put in the waste basket. I came to know it very well as I got Ford Madox Ford to publish it in *The Transatlantic Review* serially—forced, perhaps would be the word—knowing that it would outrun the life of the review. I was overly familiar with the review's finances, and I had to read all of Miss Stein's proof for her as this was a work which gave her no happiness.

On this cold afternoon when I had come past the

concierge's lodge and the cold courtyard to the warmth of the studio, all that was years ahead; and on this day Miss Stein was instructing me about sex. By that time we liked each other very much and I had already learned some time before that everything I did not understand probably had something to it. Miss Stein thought that I was what we would probably call now a square about sex and I must admit that I had certain prejudices against homosexuality since I knew its more primitive aspects. I knew it was why you carried a knife and would use it when you were in the company of tramps when you were a boy in the days when wolves was not a slang term for men obsessed by the pursuit of women. I knew many *inaccrochable* terms and phrases from Kansas City days and the mores of different parts of that city, Chicago and the lake boats. Under questioning I tried to tell Miss Stein that when you were a boy and moved in the company of men, you had to be prepared to kill a man, know how to do it and really know that you would do it in order not to be interfered with. That was the term that was *accrochable*. If you knew you would kill, other people sensed it very quickly and you were let alone; but there were certain situations you could not allow yourself to be forced into or trapped into. I could have expressed myself more vividly by using an *inaccrochable* phrase that wolves used on the lake boats, "Oh gash may be fine but one eye for mine." But I was always careful of my language with Miss Stein even when true phrases might have clarified or better expressed a prejudice.

"Yes, yes, Hemingway," she said. "But you were living in a milieu of criminals and perverts."

I did not want to argue that, although I thought that I had lived in a world such as it was and there were all kinds of people in it and I tried to understand them; but some of them I could not like and some I still hated.

"But what about the old man with beautiful manners and a great name who came to the hospital in Italy and brought me a bottle of Marsala or Campari and behaved perfectly, and then one day you would have to tell the nurse never to let that man into the room again?" I asked.

"Those people are sick and cannot help themselves and you should pity them."

"Should I pity so and so?" I asked. I gave his name but he delights so in giving it himself that I feel there is no need to give it for him.

"No. He's vicious. He's a corrupter and he's truly vicious."

"But he's supposed to be a good writer."

"He's not," she said. "He's just a showman and he corrupts for the pleasure of corruption and he leads people into other vicious practices as well. Drugs, for example."

"And in Milan the man I'm to pity was not trying to corrupt me?"

"Don't be silly. How could he hope to corrupt you? Do you corrupt a boy like you, who drinks alcohol, with a bottle of Marsala? No, he was a pitiful old man who could not help what he was doing. He was sick and he could not help it and you should pity him."

"I did at the time," I said. "But I was disappointed because he had such beautiful manners."

I took another sip of the *eau-de-vie* and pitied the old man and looked at Picasso's nude of the girl with the basket of flowers. I had not started the conversation and thought it had become a little dangerous. There were almost never any pauses in a conversation with Miss Stein, but we had paused and there was something she wanted to tell me and I filled my glass.

"You know nothing about any of this really, Hemingway," she said. "You've met known criminals and sick people and vicious people. The main thing is that the act male homosexuals commit is ugly and repugnant and afterwards they are disgusted with themselves. They drink, take drugs, to palliate this, but they are disgusted with the act and they are always changing partners and cannot be really happy."

"I see."

"In women it is the opposite. They do nothing that they are disgusted by and nothing that is repulsive and afterwards they are happy and they can lead happy lives together."

"I see," I said. "But what about so and so?"

"She's vicious," Miss Stein said. "She's truly vicious, so she can never be happy except with new people. She corrupts people."

"I understand."

"You're sure you understand?"

There were so many things to understand in those days and I was glad when we talked about something else. The park was closed so I had to walk down along it to the rue de Vaugirard and around the lower end of the park. It was sad when the park was closed and locked and I was sad walking around it instead of through it and in a hurry to get home to the rue Cardinal Lemoine. The day had started out very brightly too. I would have to work hard tomorrow. Work could cure almost anything, I believed then, and I believe it now. Then all I had to be cured of, I believed Miss Stein felt, was youth and loving my wife. I was not at all sad when I got home to the rue Cardinal Lemoine and told my newly acquired knowledge to my wife and we were happy in the night with our own knowledge we already had and other new knowledge we had acquired in the mountains.

3

Shakespeare and Company

In those days there was no money to buy books. Books you borrowed from the rental library of Shakespeare and Company, which was the library and bookstore of Sylvia Beach at 12 rue de l'Odéon. On a cold windswept street, this was a lovely, warm, cheerful place with a big stove in winter, tables and shelves of books, new books in the window, and photographs on the wall of famous writers both dead and living. The photographs all looked like snapshots and even the dead writers looked as though they had really been alive. Sylvia had a lively, very sharply cut face, brown eyes that were as alive as a small animal's and as gay as a young girl's, and wavy brown hair that was brushed back from her fine forehead and cut thick below her ears and at the line of the collar of the brown velvet jacket she wore. She had pretty legs and she was kind, cheerful and interested, and loved to make jokes and gossip. No one that I ever knew was nicer to me.

I was very shy when I first went into the bookshop and I did not have enough money on me to join the rental library. She told me I could pay the deposit any time I had the money and made me out a card and said I could take as many books as I wished.

There was no reason for her to trust me. She did not know me and the address I had given her, 74 rue Cardinal Lemoine, could not have been a poorer one. But she was delightful and charming and welcoming and behind her, as high as the wall and stretching out into the back room which gave onto the inner court of the building, were the shelves and shelves of the richness of the library.

I started with Turgenev and took the two volumes of *A Sportsman's Sketches* and an early book of D. H. Lawrence, I think it was *Sons and Lovers,* and Sylvia told me to take more books if I wanted. I chose the Constance Garnett edition of *War and Peace,* and *The Gambler and Other Stories* by Dostoyevsky.

"You won't be back very soon if you read all that," Sylvia said.

"I'll be by to pay," I said. "I have some money in the flat."

"I didn't mean that," she said. "You pay whenever it's convenient."

"When does Joyce come in?" I asked.

"If he comes in, it's usually very late in the afternoon," she said. "Haven't you ever seen him?"

"We've seen him at Michaud's eating with his family," I said. "But it's not polite to look at someone when they are eating, and Michaud's is expensive."

"Do you eat at home?"

"Mostly now," I said. "We have a good cook."

"There aren't any restaurants in your immediate quarter, are there?"

"No. How did you know?"

"Larbaud lived there," she said. "He liked it very much except for that."

"The nearest good cheap place to eat is over by the Panthéon."

"I don't know that quarter. We eat at home. You and your wife must come sometime."

"Wait until you see if I pay you," I said. "But thank you very much."

"Don't read too fast," she said.

At home in our two-room flat that had no hot water and no inside toilet facilities except an antiseptic portable container that was not uncomfortable to anyone who was used to a Michigan outhouse, but which was a cheerful gay flat with a fine view and a good mattress and springs for a comfortable bed on the floor, well and tastefully covered, and pictures that we liked on the walls, I told my wife about the wonderful place I had found.

"But Tatie, you must go by this afternoon and pay," she said.

"Sure I will," I said. "We'll both go. And then we'll walk down by the river and along the quais."

"Let's walk down the rue de Seine and look in all the galleries and in the windows of the shops."

"Sure. We can walk anywhere and we can stop at some new café where we don't know anyone and nobody knows us and have a drink."

"We can have two drinks."

"Then we can eat somewhere."

"No. Don't forget we have to pay the library."

"We'll come home and eat here and we'll have a lovely meal and drink Beaune from the co-operative you can see right out of the window there with the price of the Beaune on the window. And afterwards we'll read and then go to bed and make love."

"And we'll never love anyone else but each other."

"No. Never."

"What a lovely afternoon and evening. Now we'd better have lunch."

"I'm very hungry," I said. "I worked at the café on a *café crème*."

"How did it go, Tatie?"

"I think all right. I hope so. What do we have for lunch?"

"Little radishes, and good *foie de veau* with mashed pota-toes and an endive salad. Apple tart."

"And we're going to have all the books in the world to read and when we go on trips we can take them."

"Would that be honest?"

"Sure."

"Does she have Henry James too?"

"Sure."

"My," she said. "We're lucky that you found the place."

"We're always lucky," I said and like a fool I did not knock on wood. There was wood everywhere in that apartment to knock on too.

4

People of the Seine

There were many ways of walking down to the river from the top of the rue Cardinal Lemoine where we lived. The shortest one was straight down the street but it was steep and it brought you out, after you hit the flat part and crossed the busy traffic of the beginning of the Boulevard St.-Germain, onto a dull part where there was a dull, windy stretch of river bank with the Halle aux Vins on your right. This was not like any other Paris market but was a sort of bonded warehouse where wine was stored against the payment of taxes and was as cheerless from the outside as a military depot or a prison camp.

Across the branch of the Seine was the Île St.-Louis with the narrow streets and the old, tall, beautiful houses, and you could go over there or you could turn left and walk along the quais with the length of the Île St.-Louis and then Notre-Dame and Île de la Cité opposite as you walked.

In the bookstalls along the quais you could sometimes find American books that had just been published for sale very cheaply. The Tour D'Argent restaurant had a few rooms above the restaurant that they rented in those days, giving the people who lived there a discount in the restaurant, and if the people who lived there left any books behind there was a bookstall not far along the quai where the *valet de chambre* sold them and you could buy them from the proprietress for a very few francs. She had no confidence in books written in

English, paid almost nothing for them, and sold them for a small and quick profit.

"Are they any good?" she asked me after we had become friends.

"Sometimes one is."

"How can anyone tell?"

"I can tell when I read them."

"But still it is a form of gambling. And how many people can read English?"

"Save them for me and let me look them over."

"No. I can't save them. You don't pass regularly. You stay away too long at a time. I have to sell them as soon as I can. No one can tell if they are worthless. If they turn out to be worthless, I would never sell them."

"How do you tell a valuable French book?"

"First there are the pictures. Then it is a question of the quality of the pictures. Then it is the binding. If a book is good, the owner will have it bound properly. All books in English are bound, but bound badly. There is no way of judging them."

After that bookstall near the Tour D'Argent there were no others that sold American and English books until the quai des Grands Augustins. There were several from there on to past the quai Voltaire that sold books they bought from employees of the left bank hotels and especially the Hotel Voltaire which had a wealthier clientele than most. One day I asked another woman stall-keeper who was a friend of mine if the owners ever sold the books.

"No," she said. "They are all thrown away. That is why one knows they have no value."

"Friends give them to them to read on the boats."

"Doubtless," she said. "They must leave many on the boats."

"They do," I said. "The line keeps them and binds them and they become the ships' libraries."

"That's intelligent," she said. "At least they are properly bound then. Now a book like that would have value."

I would walk along the quais when I had finished work or when I was trying to think something out. It was easier to think if I was walking and doing something or seeing people doing something that they understood. At the head of the Île de la Cité below the Pont Neuf where there was the statue of Henri Quatre, the island ended in a point like the sharp bow of a ship and there was a small park at the water's edge with fine chestnut trees, some huge and spreading, and in the currents and back waters that the Seine made flowing past, there were excellent places to fish. You went down a stairway to the park and watched the fishermen there and under the great bridge. The good spots to fish changed with the height of the river and the fishermen used long, jointed, cane poles but fished with very fine leaders and light gear and quill floats and baited the piece of water that they fished expertly. They always caught some fish, and often they made excellent catches of the dace-like fish that were called *goujon*. They were delicious fried whole and I could eat a plateful. They were plump and sweet-fleshed with a finer flavor than fresh sardines even, and were not at all oily, and we ate them bones and all.

One of the best places to eat them was at an open-air restaurant built out over the river at Bas Meudon where we would go when we had money for a trip away from our quarter. It was called La Pêche Miraculeuse and had a splendid white wine that was a sort of Muscadet. It was a place out of a Maupassant story with the view over the river as Sisley had painted it. You did not have to go that far to eat *goujon*. You could get a very good *friture* on the Île St.-Louis.

I knew several of the men who fished the fruitful parts of the Seine between the Île St.-Louis and the Square du Vert Galent and sometimes, if the day was bright, I would buy a liter of wine and a piece of bread and some sausage and sit in the sun and read one of the books I had bought and watch the fishing.

Travel writers wrote about the men fishing in the Seine as though they were crazy and never caught anything; but it was serious and productive fishing. Most of the fishermen were men who had small pensions, which they did not know then would become worthless with inflation, or keen fishermen who fished on their days or half-days off from work. There was better fishing at Charenton, where the Marne came into the Seine, and on either side of Paris, but there was very good fishing in Paris itself. I did not fish because I did not have the tackle and I would rather save my money to fish in Spain. Then too I never knew when I would be through working, nor when I would have to be away, and I did not want to become involved in the fishing which had its good times and its slack times. But I followed it closely and it was interesting and good to know about, and it always made me happy that there were men fishing in the city itself, having sound, serious fishing and taking a few *fritures* home to their families.

With the fishermen and the life on the river, the beautiful barges with their own life on board, the tugs with their smokestacks that folded back to pass under the bridges, pulling a tow of barges, the great plain trees on the stone banks of the river, the elms and sometimes the poplars, I could never be lonely along the river. With so many trees in the city, you could see the spring coming each day until a night of warm wind would bring it suddenly in one morning. Sometimes the heavy cold rains would beat it back so that it would seem that it would never come and that you were losing a season out of your life. This was the only truly sad time in Paris because it was unnatural. You expected to be sad in the fall. Part of you died each year when the leaves fell from the trees and their branches were bare against the wind and the cold, wintry light. But you knew there would always be the spring, as you knew the river would flow again after it was frozen. When the cold rains kept on and killed the spring, it was as though a young person had died for no reason.

In those days, though, the spring always came finally; but it was frightening that it had nearly failed.

5

A False Spring

When spring came, even the false spring, there were no problems except where to be happiest. The only thing that could spoil a day was people and if you could keep from making engagements, each day had no limits. People were always the limiters of happiness except for the very few that were as good as spring itself.

In the spring mornings I would work early while my wife still slept. The windows were open wide and the cobbles of the street were drying after the rain. The sun was drying the wet faces of the houses that faced the window. The shops were still shuttered. The goatherd came up the street blowing his pipes and a woman who lived on the floor above us came out onto the sidewalk with a big pot. The goatherd chose one of the heavy-bagged, black milk-goats and milked her into the pot while his dog pushed the others onto the sidewalk. The goats looked around, turning their necks like sight-seers. The goatherd took the money from the woman and thanked her and went on up the street piping and the dog herded the goats on ahead, their horns bobbing. I went back to writing and the woman came up the stairs with the goat milk. She wore her felt-soled cleaning shoes and I only heard her breathing as she stopped on the stairs outside our door and then the shutting of her door. She was the only customer for goat milk in our building.

I thought I would go down and buy a morning racing

paper. There was no quarter too poor to have at least one copy of a racing paper but you had to buy it early on a day like this. I found one in the rue Descartes at the corner of the Place Contrescarpe. The goats were going down the rue Descartes and I breathed the air in and walked back fast to climb the stairs and get my work done. I had been tempted to stay out and follow the goats down the early morning street. But before I started again I looked at the paper. They were running at Enghien, the small, pretty and larcenous track that was the home of the outsider.

So that day after I had finished work we would go racing. Some money had come from the Toronto paper that I did newspaper work for and we wanted a long shot if we could find one. My wife had a horse one time at Auteuil named Chèvre d'Or that was a hundred and twenty to one and leading by twenty lengths when he fell at the last jump with enough savings on him to ——. We tried never to think to do what. We were ahead on that year but Chèvre d'Or would have ——. We didn't think about Chèvre d'Or.

"Do we have enough money to really bet, Tatie?" my wife asked.

"No. We'll just figure to spend what we take. Is there something else you'd rather spend it for?"

"Well," she said.

"I know. It's been terribly hard and I've been tight and mean about money."

"No," she said. "But—"

I knew how severe I had been and how bad things had been. The one who is doing his work and getting satisfaction from it is not the one the poverty is hard on. I thought of bathtubs and showers and toilets that flushed as things that inferior people to us had or that you enjoyed when you made trips, which we often made. There was always the public bathhouse down at the foot of the street by the river. My wife had never complained once about these things any more than she cried about Chèvre d'Or when he fell. She had cried for the horse, I remembered; but not for the money. I had been stupid when she needed a grey lamb jacket and had loved it once she had bought it. I had been stupid about other things too. It was all part of the fight against poverty that you never win except by not spending. Especially if you buy pictures instead of clothes. But then we did not think ever of ourselves as poor. We did not accept it. We thought we were superior people and other people that we looked down on and rightly mistrusted were rich. It had never seemed strange to me later on to wear sweatshirts for underwear to keep warm. It only seemed odd to the rich. We ate well and cheaply and drank well and cheaply and slept well and warm together and loved each other.

"I think we ought to go," my wife said. "We haven't been for such a long time. We'll take a lunch and some wine. I'll make good sandwiches."

"We'll go on the train and it's cheap that way. But let's not go if you don't think we should. Anything we'd do today would be fun. It's a wonderful day."

"I think we should go."

"You wouldn't rather spend it some other way?"

"No," she said arrogantly. She had the lovely high cheekbones for arrogance. "Who are we anyway?"

So we went out by the train from the Gare du Nord through the dirtiest and saddest part of town and walked from the siding to the oasis of the track. It was early and we sat on my raincoat on the fresh cropped grass bank and had our lunch and drank from the wine bottle and looked at the old grandstand, the brown wooden betting booths, the green of the track, the darker green of the hurdles, and the brown shine of the water jumps and the whitewashed stone walls and white posts and rails, the paddock under the new leafed trees and the first horses being walked to the paddock. We drank more wine and studied the form in the paper and my wife lay down on the raincoat to sleep with the sun on her face. I went over and found someone I knew from the old days at San Siro in Milano. He gave me two horses.

"Mind, they're no investment. But don't let the price put you off."

We won the first with half of the money that we had to spend and he paid twelve to one, jumping beautifully, taking command on the far side of the course and coming in four lengths ahead. We saved half of the money and put it away and bet the other half on the second horse who broke ahead, led all the way over the hurdles and on the flat just lasted to the finish line with the favorite gaining on him with every jump and the two whips flailing.

We went to have a glass of champagne at the bar under the stand and wait for the prices to go up.

"My, but racing is very hard on people," my wife said. "Did you see that horse come up on him?"

"I can still feel it inside me."

"What will he pay?"

"The *cote* was eighteen to one. But they may have bet him at the last."

The horses came by, ours wet, with his nostrils working wide to breathe; the jockey patting him.

"Poor him," my wife said. "We just bet."

We watched them go on by and had another glass of champagne and then the winning came up: 85. That meant he paid eighty-five francs for ten.

"They must have put a lot of money on at the end," I said.

But we had made plenty of money, big money for us, and now we had spring and money too. I thought that was all we needed. A day like that one, if you split the winnings one quarter for each to spend, left a half for racing capital. I kept the racing capital secret and apart from all other capital and there was racing at some track every day.

Another day later that year when we had come back from one of our voyages and had good luck at some track again we stopped at Pruniers on the way home, going in to sit at the bar after looking at all the clearly priced wonders in the window. We had oysters and *crabe Mexicaine* with glasses of Sancerre. We walked back through the Tuileries in the dark and stood and looked through the Arc du Carrousel up across the dark gardens with the lights of the Concorde behind the formal darkness and then the long rise of lights toward the Arc de Triomphe. Then we looked back toward the dark of the Louvre and I said, "Do you really think that the three arches are in line? These two and the Sermione in Milano?"

"I don't know, Tatie. They say so and they ought to know. Do you remember when we came out into the spring on the Italian side of the St. Bernard after the climb in the snow, and you and Chink and I walked down all day in the spring to Aosta?"

"Chink called it 'across the St. Bernard in street shoes.' Remember your shoes?"

"My poor shoes. Do you remember us having fruit cup at Biffi's in the Galleria with Capri and fresh peaches and wild strawberries in a tall glass pitcher with ice?"

"That time was what made me wonder about the three arches."

"I remember the Sermione. It's like this arch."

"Do you remember the Aigle where you and Chink sat in the garden that day and read while I fished?"

"Yes, Tatie."

I remembered the Rhône, narrow and grey and full of snow water and the two trout streams on either side, the Stockalper and the Rhône canal. The Stockalper was really clear that day and the Rhône canal was still murky.

"Do you remember when the horse-chestnut trees were in bloom and how I tried to remember a story that Jim Gamble, I think, had told me about a wisteria vine and I couldn't remember it?"

"Yes Tatie, and you and Chink always talking about how to make things true, writing them, and put them rightly and not describe. I remember everything. Sometimes he was right and sometimes you were right. I remember the lights and textures and the shapes you argued about."

Now we had come out of the gateway through the Louvre and crossed the street outside and were standing on the bridge leaning on the stone and looking down at the river.

"We all three argued about everything and always specific things and we made fun of each other. I remember everything we ever did and everything we ever said on the whole trip," Hadley said. "I do really. About everything. When you and Chink talked I was included. It wasn't like being a wife at Miss Stein's."

"I wish I could remember the story about the wisteria vine."

"It wasn't important. It was the vine that was important, Tatie."

"Do you remember I brought some wine from Aigle home to the chalet? They sold it to us at the inn. They said it should go with the trout. We brought it wrapped in copies of *La Gazette de Lausanne*, I think."

"The Sion wine was even better. Do you remember how Mrs. Gangeswisch cooked the trout *au bleu* when we got back to the chalet? They were such wonderful trout, Tatie, and we drank the Sion wine and ate out on the porch with the mountainside dropping off below and we could look across the lake and see the Dent du Midi with the snow half down it and the trees at the mouth of the Rhône where it flowed into the lake."

"We always miss Chink in the winter and the spring."

"Always. And I miss him now when it is gone."

Chink was a professional soldier and had gone out to Mons from Sandhurst. I had met him first in Italy and he had been my best friend and then our best friend for a long time. He spent his leaves with us then.

"He's going to try to get leave this next spring. He wrote last week from Cologne."

"I know. We should live in this time now and have every minute of it."

"We're watching the water now as it hits this buttress. Look what we can see when we look up the river."

We looked and there it all was: our river and our city and the island of our city.

"We're too lucky," she said. "I hope Chink will come. He takes care of us."

"He doesn't think so."

"Of course not."

"He thinks we explore together."

"We do. But it depends on what you explore."

We walked across the bridge and were on our own side of the river.

"Are you hungry again?" I said. "Us. Talking and walking."

"Of course, Tatie. Aren't you?"

"Let's go to a wonderful place and have a truly grand dinner."

"Where?"

"Michaud's?"

"That's perfect and it's so close."

So we walked up the rue des Saints-Pères to the corner of the rue Jacob stopping and looking in the windows at pictures and at furniture. We stood outside of Michaud's restaurant reading the posted menu. Michaud's was crowded and we waited for people to come out, watching the tables where people already had their coffee.

We were hungry again from walking and Michaud's was an exciting and expensive restaurant for us. It was where Joyce ate with his family then, he and his wife against the wall, Joyce peering at the menu through his thick glasses holding the menu up in one hand; Nora by him, a hearty but delicate eater; Giorgio thin, foppish, sleek-headed from the back; Lucia with heavy curly hair, a girl not quite yet grown; all of them talking Italian.

Standing there I wondered how much of what we had felt on the bridge was just hunger. I asked my wife and she said, "I don't know, Tatie. There are so many sorts of hunger. In the spring there are more. But that's gone now. Memory is hunger."

I was being stupid, and looking in the window and seeing two *tournedos* being served I knew I was hungry in a simple way.

"You said we were lucky today. Of course we were. But we had very good advice and information."

She laughed.

"I didn't mean about the racing. You're such a literal boy. I meant lucky in other ways."

"I don't think Chink cares for racing," I said compounding my stupidity.

"No. He'd only care for it if he were riding."

"Don't you want to go racing any more?"

"Of course. And now we can go whenever we want again."

"But you really want to go?"

"Of course. You do, don't you?"

It was a wonderful meal at Michaud's after we got in; but when we had finished and there was no question of hunger any more the feeling that had been like hunger when we were on the bridge was still there when we caught the bus home. It was there when we came in the room and after we had gone to bed and made love in the dark, it was there. When I woke with the windows open and the moonlight on the roofs of the tall houses, it was there. I put my face away from the moonlight into the shadow but I could not sleep and lay awake thinking about it. We had both wakened twice in the night and my wife slept sweetly now with the moonlight on her face. I had to try to think it out and I was too stupid. Life had seemed so simple that morning when I had wakened and found the false spring and heard the pipes of the man with his herd of goats and gone out and bought the racing paper.

But Paris was a very old city and we were young and nothing was simple there, not even poverty, nor sudden money, nor the moonlight, nor right and wrong nor the breathing of someone who lay beside you in the moonlight.

6

The End of an Avocation

We went racing together many more times that year and other years after I had worked in the early mornings, and Hadley enjoyed it and sometimes she loved it. But it was not the climbs in the high mountain meadows above the last forest, nor nights coming home to the chalet, nor was it climbing with Chink, our best friend, over a high pass into new country. It was not really racing either. It was gambling on horses. But we called it racing.

Racing never came between us, only people could do that; but for a long time it stayed close to us like a demanding friend. That was a generous way to speak of it. I, the one who was so righteous about people and their destructiveness, tolerated this one that was the falsest, most beautiful, most exciting, vicious, and demanding because she could be profitable. To make it profitable was more than a full-time job and I had no time for that. But I justified it to myself because I wrote it. Though in the end, when everything I had written was lost, there was only one racing story that was out in the mails that survived.

I was going to races alone more now and I was involved in them and getting too mixed up with them. I worked two tracks in their season when I could, Auteuil and Enghien. It took full-time work to try to handicap intelligently and you could make no money that way. That was just how it worked out on paper. You could buy a paper that gave you that.

You had to watch a jumping race from the top of the stands at Auteuil and it was a fast climb up to see what each horse did and see the horse that might have won and did not, and see why, or at least how, or maybe how he did not do what he could have done. You watched the prices and all the shifts of odds each time a horse you were following would start, and you had to know how he was working and finally get to know when the stable would try with him. He always might be beaten when he tried; but you should know by then what his chances were. It was hard work but at Auteuil it was beautiful to watch each day they raced when you could be there and see the honest races with the great horses, and you got to know the course as well as any place you had ever known. You knew many people finally, jockeys and trainers and owners and too many horses and too many things.

You only, in principle, bet when you had a horse to bet on but you sometimes found horses that nobody believed in except the men who trained and rode them that won race after race with you betting on them. You had to follow it very closely to really know anything. I stopped finally because it took too much time, I was getting too involved and I knew too much about what went on at Enghien and at the flat racing tracks too.

When I stopped working on the races I was glad but it left an emptiness. By then I knew that everything good and bad left an emptiness when it stopped. But if it was bad, the emptiness filled up by itself. If it was good you could only fill it by finding something better. I put the racing capital back into the general funds and I felt relaxed and good.

The day I gave up racing I went over to the other side of the river and met my friend Mike Ward at the travel desk in the Guaranty Trust which was then at the corner of the rue des Italiens on the Boulevard des Italiens. I was depositing the racing capital but I did not tell that to anyone. I didn't put it in the checkbook though I still kept it in my head.

"Want to go to lunch?" I asked Mike.

"Sure, kid. Yeah I can do it. What's the matter? Aren't you going to the track?"

"No."

We had lunch at the square Louvois at a very good, plain bistro with a wonderful white wine. Across the square was the Bibliothèque Nationale.

"You never went to the track much, Mike," I said.

"No. Not for quite a long time."

"Why did you lay off it?"

"I don't know," Mike said. "Yes. Sure I do. Anything you have to bet on to get a kick isn't worth seeing."

"Don't you ever go out?"

"Sometimes to see a big race. One with great horses."

We spread paté on the good bistro bread and drank the white wine.

"Did you follow them a lot, Mike?"

"Oh yes."

"What do you see that's better?"

"Bicycle racing."

"Really?"

"You don't have to bet on it. You'll see."

"That track takes a lot of time."

"Too much time. Takes all your time. I don't like the people."

"I was very interested."

"Sure. You make out all right?"

"All right."

"Good thing to stop," Mike said.

"I've stopped."

"Hard to do. Listen kid, we'll go to the bike races sometime."

That was a new and fine thing that I knew little about. But we did not start it right away. That came later. It came to be a big part of our lives later when the first part of Paris was broken up.

But for a long time it was enough just to be back in our part of Paris and away from the track and to bet on your own life and work, and on the painters that you knew and not try to make your living gambling and call it by some other name. I have started many stories about bicycle racing but have never written one that is as good as it is both on the indoor and outdoor tracks and on the roads. All that and the six day races are still to come. But I will get the Vélodrome d'Hiver with the smoky light of the afternoon and the high-banked wooden track and the whirring sound the tires made on the wood as the riders passed, the effort and the tactics as the riders climbed and plunged, each one a part of his machine; I will get the magic of the *demi-fond*, the noise of the motors with their rollers set out behind them that the *entraîneurs* rode, wearing their heavy crash helmets and leaning backward in their ponderous leather suits, to shelter the riders who followed them from the air resistance, the riders in their lighter crash helmets bent low over their handlebars their legs turning the huge gear sprockets and the small front wheels touching the roller behind the machine that gave them a shelter from the air resistance to ride in, and the duels that were more exciting than any racing, the *put-put*ing of the motorcycles and the riders elbow to elbow and wheel to wheel up and down and around at deadly speed until one man could not hold the pace and broke away and the solid wall of air that he had been sheltered against hit him.

There were so many kinds of racing. The straight sprints

raced in heats or in match races where the two riders would balance for long seconds on their machines for the advantage of making the other rider take the lead and then the slow circling and the final plunge into the driving purity of speed. There were the programs of the team races of two hours, with a series of pure sprints in their heats to fill the afternoon, the lonely absolute speed events of one man racing an hour against the clock, the terribly dangerous and beautiful races of one hundred kilometers on the big banked wooden five-hundred-meter bowl of the Stade Buffalo, the outdoor stadium at Montrouge where they raced behind big motorcycles, Linart, the great Belgian champion that they called "the Sioux" for his profile, dropping his head to suck up cherry brandy from a rubber tube that connected with a hot water bottle under his racing shirt when he needed it toward the end as he increased his savage speed, and the championships of France behind big motors of the six-hundred-and-sixty-meter cement track of the Parc du Prince near Auteuil, the wickedest track of all where Pauline and I saw that great rider Ganay fall and heard his skull crumple under the crash helmet as you crack an hard-boiled egg against a stone to peel it on a picnic. I must write the strange world of the six-day races and the marvels of the road-racing in the mountains. French is the only language it has ever been written in properly and the terms are all French and that is what makes it so hard to write. But Mike was right about it, there is no need to bet and it comes at another time in Paris.

7

"Une Génération Perdue"

It was easy to get into the habit of stopping in at 27 rue de Fleurus late in the afternoon for the warmth and the great pictures and the conversation. Often Miss Stein would have no guests and she was always very friendly and for a long time she was affectionate. She loved to talk about people and places and things and food. When I had come back from trips that I had made to the different political conferences or to the Near East or Germany for the Canadian paper and the news services that I did work for she wanted me to tell her about all the amusing things that had happened. There were funny things always and she liked them and also what the Germans call gallows-humor stories. She did not like to hear really bad nor tragic things, but no one does, and having seen them I did not care to talk about them unless she wanted to know how the world was going. She wanted to know the gay part of how the world was going; never the real, never the bad.

I was young and not gloomy and there were always strange and comic things that happened in the worst time and Miss Stein liked to hear these things. The other things I did not talk of and wrote by myself.

When I had not come back from any trips and would stop in at the rue de Fleurus after working I would try sometimes to get Miss Stein to talk about books. When I was writing, it was necessary for me to read after I had written, to keep my mind from going on with the story I was working on. If you kept thinking about it, you would lose the thing that you were writing before you could go on with it the next day. It was necessary to get exercise, to be tired in my body, and it was very good to make love with whom you loved. That was better than anything. But afterwards, when you were empty, it was necessary to read in order not to think or worry about your work until you could do it again. I had learned already never to empty the well of my writing; but always to stop when there was still something there in the deep part of the well, and let it refill at night from the springs that fed it.

To keep my mind off writing sometimes after I had worked I would read writers who were writing then, such as Aldous Huxley, D. H. Lawrence or any who had books published that you could get from Sylvia Beach's library or find along the quais.

"Huxley is a dead man," Miss Stein said. "Why do you want to read a dead man? Can't you see he is dead?"

I could not see, then, that he was a dead man and I said that his books amused me and kept me from thinking.

"You should only read what is truly good or what is frankly bad."

"I've been reading truly good books all winter and all last winter and I'll read them next winter, and I don't like frankly bad books."

"Why do you read this trash? It is inflated trash, Hemingway. By a dead man."

"I like to see what they are writing," I said. "And it keeps my mind off me doing it."

"Who else do you read now?"

"D. H. Lawrence," I said. "He wrote some very good short stories, one called 'The Prussian Officer.'"

"I tried to read his novels. He's impossible. He's pathetic and preposterous. He writes like a sick man."

"I liked *Sons and Lovers* and *The White Peacock*," I said. "Maybe that not so well. I couldn't read *Women in Love*."

"If you don't want to read what is bad, and want to read something that will hold your interest and is marvelous in its own way, you should read Marie Belloc Lowndes."

I had never heard of her, and Miss Stein loaned me *The Lodger*, that marvelous story of Jack the Ripper and another book about murder at a place outside Paris that could only be Enghien les Bains. They were both splendid after-work books, the people credible and the action and the terror never false. They were perfect for reading after you had worked and I read all the Mrs. Belloc Lowndes that there was. But there was only so much and none as good as the first two and I never found anything as good for that empty time of day or night until the first fine Simenon books came out.

I think Miss Stein would have liked the good Simenons— the first one I read was either *L'Ecluse Numéro 1*, or *La Maison du Canal*—but I am not sure because when I knew Miss Stein she did not like to read French although she loved to speak it. Janet Flanner gave me the first two Simenons I ever read. She loved to read French and she had read Simenon when he was a crime reporter.

In the three or four years that we were good friends I cannot remember Gertrude Stein ever speaking well of any writer who had not written favorably about her work or done something to advance her career except for Ronald Firbank and, later, Scott Fitzgerald. When I first met her she did not speak of Sherwood Anderson as a writer but spoke glowingly of him as a man and of his great, beautiful, warm Italian eyes and of his kindness and his charm. I did not care about his great beautiful warm Italian eyes but I liked some of his short stories very much. They were simply written and sometimes beautifully written and he knew the people he was writing about and cared deeply for them. Miss Stein did not want to talk about his stories but always about him as a person.

"What about his novels?" I asked her. She did not want to talk about Anderson's works any more than she would talk about Joyce. If you brought up Joyce twice, you would not be invited back. It was like mentioning one general favorably to another general. You learned not to do it the first time you made the mistake. You could always mention a general, though, that the general you were talking to had beaten. The general you were talking to would praise the beaten general greatly and go happily into detail on how he had beaten him.

Anderson's stories were too good to make happy conversation. I was prepared to tell Miss Stein how strangely poor his novels were, but this would have been bad too because it was criticizing one of her most loyal supporters. When he wrote a novel finally called *Dark Laughter,* so terribly bad, silly and affected that I could not keep from criticizing it in a parody,* Miss Stein was very angry. I had attacked some-one that was a part of her apparatus. But for a long time before that she was not angry. She, herself, began to praise Sherwood lavishly after he had cracked up as a writer.

She was angry at Ezra Pound because he had sat down too quickly on a small, fragile and, doubtless, uncomfortable chair, that it is quite possible he had been given on pur-pose, and had either cracked or broken it. That finished Ezra at 27 rue de Fleurus. That he was a great poet and a gentle and generous man and could have accommodated himself in a normal-size chair was not considered. The rea-sons for her dislike of Ezra, skillfully and maliciously put, were invented years later.

* The Torrents of Spring

It was when we had come back from Canada and while we were living in the rue Notre-Dame-des-Champs and Miss Stein and I were still good friends that Miss Stein made the remark about the lost generation. She had some ignition trouble with the old Model T Ford she then drove and the young man who worked in the garage and had served in the last year of the war had not been adept, or perhaps had not broken the priority of other vehicles, in repairing Miss Stein's Ford. Perhaps he had not realized the importance of Miss Stein's vehicle having the right of immediate repair. Anyway he had not been *sérieux* and had been corrected severely by the *patron* of the garage after Miss Stein's protest. The *patron* had said to him, "You are all a *génération perdue*."

"That's what you are. That's what you all are," Miss Stein said. "All of you young people who served in the war. You are a lost generation."

"Really?" I said.

"You are," she insisted. "You have no respect for anything. You drink yourselves to death. . . ."

"Was the young mechanic drunk?" I asked.

"Of course not."

"Have you ever seen me drunk?"

"No. But your friends are drunk."

"I've been drunk," I said. "But I don't come here drunk."

"Of course not. I didn't say that."

"The boy's *patron* was probably drunk by eleven o'clock in the morning," I said. "That's why he makes such lovely phrases."

"Don't argue with me, Hemingway," Miss Stein said. "It does no good at all. You're all a lost generation, exactly as the garage keeper said."

Later when I published my first novel I tried to balance Miss Stein's quotation from the garage keeper with one from Ecclesiastes. But that night walking home I thought about the boy in the garage and if he had ever been hauled in one of those vehicles when they were converted to ambulances. I remembered how they used to burn out their brakes going down the mountain roads with a full load of wounded and braking in low and finally using the reverse, and how the last ones were driven over the mountainside empty, so they could be replaced by big Fiats with a good H-shift and metal-to-metal brakes. I thought of Miss Stein and Sherwood Anderson and egotism and mental laziness versus discipline and I thought who is calling who a lost generation? Then as I was getting up to the Closerie des Lilas with the light on my old friend, the statue of Marshal Ney with his sword out and the shadows of the trees on the bronze, and he alone there and nobody behind him and what a balls-up he'd made of Waterloo, I thought that all generations were lost by something and always had been and always would be and I stopped at the Lilas to keep the statue company and drank a cold beer before going home to the flat over the sawmill. But sitting there with the beer, watching the statue and remembering how many days Ney had fought, personally, with the rearguard on the retreat from Moscow that Napoleon had ridden away from in the coach with Caulaincourt, I thought of what a warm and affectionate friend Miss Stein had been and how beautifully she had spoken of Apollinaire and of his death on the day of the Armistice in 1918 with the crowd shouting "*à bas Guillaume*" and Apollinaire, in his delirium, thinking they were crying against him, and I thought, I will do my best to serve her and see she gets justice for the good work she had done as long as I can, so help me God and Mike Ney. But the hell with her lost-generation talk and all the dirty, easy labels.

When I got home and into the courtyard and upstairs and

saw my wife and my son and his cat, F. Puss, all of them happy and a fire in the fireplace, I said to my wife, "You know, Gertrude *is* nice, anyway."

"Of course, Tatie."

"But she does talk a lot of rot sometimes."

"I never hear her," my wife said. "I'm a wife. It's her friend that talks to me."

8

Hunger Was Good Discipline

You got very hungry when you did not eat enough in Paris because all the bakery shops had such good things in the windows and people ate outside at tables on the sidewalk so that you saw and smelled the food. When you were skipping meals at a time when you had given up journalism and were writing nothing that anyone in America would buy, explaining at home that you were lunching out with someone, the best place to do it was the Luxembourg gardens where you saw and smelled nothing to eat all the way from the Place de l'Observatoire to the rue de Vaugirard. There you could always go into the Luxembourg museum and all the paintings were heightened and clearer and more beautiful if you were belly-empty, hollow-hungry. I learned to understand Cézanne much better and to see truly how he made landscapes when I was hungry. I used to wonder if he were hungry too when he painted; but I thought it was possibly only that he had forgotten to eat. It was one of those unsound but illuminating thoughts you have when you have been sleepless or hungry. Later I thought Cézanne was probably hungry in a different way.

After you came out of the Luxembourg you could walk down the narrow rue Férou to the Place St.-Sulpice and there were still no restaurants, only the quiet square with its benches and trees. There was a fountain with lions, and pigeons walked on the pavement and perched on the statues of the bishops. There was the church and there were shops selling religious objects and vestments on the north side of the square.

From this square you could not go further toward the river without passing shops selling fruits, vegetables, wines, or bakery and pastry shops. But by choosing your way carefully you could work to your right around the grey and white stone church and reach the rue de l'Odéon and turn up to your right toward Sylvia Beach's bookshop and on your way you did not pass too many places where things to eat were sold. The rue de l'Odéon was bare of eating places until you reached the square where there were three restaurants.

By the time you reached 12 rue de l'Odéon your hunger was contained but all of your perceptions were heightened again. The photographs looked different and you saw books that you had never seen before.

"You're too thin, Hemingway," Sylvia would say. "Are you eating enough?"

"Sure."

"What did you eat for lunch?"

My stomach would turn over and I would say, "I'm going home for lunch now."

"At three o'clock?"

"I didn't know it was that late."

"Adrienne said the other night she wanted to have you and Hadley for dinner. We'd ask Fargue. You like Fargue, don't you? Or Larbaud. You like him. I know you like him. Or anyone you really like. Will you speak to Hadley?"

"I know she'd love to come."

"I'll send her a *pneu*. Don't you work so hard now that you don't eat properly."

"I won't."

"Get home now before it's too late for lunch."

"They'll save it."

"Don't eat cold food either. Eat a good hot lunch."

"Did I have any mail?"

"I don't think so. But let me look."

She looked and found a note and looked up happily and then opened a closed door in her desk.

"This came while I was out," she said. It was a letter and it felt as though it had money in it. "Wedderkop," Sylvia said.

"It must be from *Der Querschnitt*. Did you see Wedderkop?"

"No. But he was here with George. He'll see you. Don't worry. Perhaps he wanted to pay you first."

"It's six hundred francs. He says there will be more."

"I'm awfully glad you reminded me to look. Dear Mr. Awfully Nice."

"It's damned funny that Germany is the only place I can sell anything. To him and the *Frankfurter Zeitung*."

"Isn't it? But don't you worry ever. You can sell stories to Ford," she teased me.

"Thirty francs a page. Say one story every three months in *the transatlantic*. Story five pages long make one hundred and fifty francs a quarter. Six hundred francs a year."

"But, Hemingway, don't worry about what they bring now. The point is that you can write them."

"I know. I can write them. But nobody will buy them. There is no money coming in since I quit journalism."

"They will sell. Look. You have the money for one right there."

"I'm sorry, Sylvia. You forgive me for speaking about it."

"Forgive you for what? Always talk about it or about anything. Don't you know all writers ever talk about is their troubles? But promise me you won't worry and that you'll eat enough."

"I promise."

"Then get home now and have lunch."

Outside on the rue de l'Odéon I was disgusted with myself for having complained about things. I was doing what I did of my own free will and I was doing it stupidly. I should have bought a large piece of bread and eaten it instead of skipping a meal. I could taste the brown lovely crust. But it is dry in your mouth without something to drink. You God damn complainer. You dirty phony saint and martyr, I said to myself. You quit journalism of your own accord. You have credit and Sylvia would have loaned you money. She has plenty of times. Sure. And then the next thing you would be compromising on something else. Hunger is healthy and the pictures do look better when you are hungry. Eating is wonderful too and do you know where you are going to eat right now?

Lipp's is where you are going to eat and drink too.

It was a quick walk to Lipp's and every place I passed that my stomach noticed as quickly as my eyes or my nose made the walk an added pleasure. There were few people in the *brasserie* and when I sat down on the bench against the wall with the mirror in back and a table in front and the waiter asked if I wanted beer I asked for a *distingué*, the big glass mug that held a liter, and for potato salad.

The beer was very cold and wonderful to drink. The *pommes à l'huile* were firm and marinated and the olive oil delicious. I ground black pepper over the potatoes and moistened the bread in the olive oil. After the first heavy draft of beer I drank and ate very slowly. When the *pommes à l'huile* were gone I ordered another serving and a *cervelas*. This was a sausage like a heavy, wide frankfurter split in two and covered with a special mustard sauce.

I mopped up all the oil and all of the sauce with bread and drank the beer slowly until it began to lose its coldness and then I finished it and ordered a *demi* and watched it drawn. It seemed colder than the *distingué* and I drank half of it.

I had not been worrying, I thought. I knew the stories were good and someone would publish them finally at home. When I stopped doing newspaper work I was sure the stories were going to be published. But every one I sent out came back. What had made me so confident was Edward O'Brien's taking the "My Old Man" story for the *Best Short Stories* book and then dedicating the book for that year to me. Then I laughed and drank some more beer. The story had never been published in a magazine and he had broken all his rules to take it for the book. I laughed again and the waiter glanced at me. It was funny because, after all that, he had spelled the name wrong. It was one of two stories I had left when everything I had written was stolen in Hadley's suitcase that time at the Gare de Lyon when she was bringing the manuscripts down to me to Lausanne as a surprise. So I could work on them on our holidays in the mountains. She had put in the originals, the typescripts and the carbons, all in these manila folders. The only reason I had the one story was that Lincoln Steffens had sent it out to some editor who sent it back. It was in the mail while everything else was stolen. The other story that I had was the one called "Up in Michigan" written before Miss Stein had come to our flat that I had never had copied because she said it was *inaccrochable*. It had been in a drawer somewhere.

So after we had left Lausanne and gone down to Italy I showed the racing story to O'Brien, a gentle, shy man, pale, with pale blue eyes, and straight lanky hair he cut himself, who lived then as a boarder in a monastery up above Rapallo. It was a bad time and I did not think I could write any more then, and I showed the story to him as a curiosity, as you might show, stupidly, the binnacle of a ship you had lost in some incredible way, or as you might pick up your booted foot if it had been amputated after a crash and make some joke about it. Then, when he read the story, I saw he was hurt far more than I was. I had never seen anyone hurt by a thing other than death or unbearable suffering except Hadley when she told me about the things being gone. She had cried and cried and could not tell me. I told her that no matter what the dreadful thing was that had happened nothing could be that bad, and whatever it was, it was all right and not to worry. We would work it out. Then, finally, she told me. I was sure she could not have brought the carbons too and I hired someone to cover for me on my newspaper job, I was making good money then at journalism, and took the train for Paris. It was true all right and I remember what I did in the night after I let myself into the flat and found it was true. That was over now and Chink had taught me never to discuss casualties so I told O'Brien not to feel so badly. It was probably good for me to lose early work and I told him all that stuff you feed the troops. I was going to start writing stories again I said and, as I said it, only trying to lie so that he would not feel so badly, I knew that it was true.

Then I started to think in Lipp's about when I had first been able to write a story after losing everything. It was up in Cortina d'Ampezzo when I had come back to join Hadley there after the spring skiing which I had to interrupt to go on assignment to the Rhineland and the Ruhr. It was a very simple story called "Out of Season" and I had omitted the real end of it which was that the old man hanged himself. This was omitted on my new theory that you could omit anything if you knew that you omitted and the omitted part would strengthen the story and make people feel something more than they understood.

Well, I thought, now I have them so they do not understand them. There cannot be much doubt about that. There is most certainly no demand for them. But they will understand the same way that they always do in painting. It only takes time and it only needs confidence.

It is necessary to handle yourself better when you have to cut down on food so you will not get too much hunger-thinking. Hunger is good discipline and you learn from it; but you can work something out. And as long as they do not understand it you are ahead of them. Oh sure, I thought, I'm so far ahead of them now that I can't afford to eat regularly. It would not be bad if they caught up a little.

I knew I must write a novel. But it seemed an impossible thing to do when I had been trying with great difficulty to write paragraphs that would be the distillation of what made a novel. It was necessary to write longer stories now as you would train for a longer race. When I had written a novel before, the one that had been lost in the bag stolen at the Gare de Lyon, I still had the lyric facility of boyhood that was as perishable and as deceptive as youth was. I knew it was probably a good thing that it was lost, but I knew too that I must write a novel. I would put it off though until I could not help doing it. I was damned if I would write one because it was what I should do if we were to eat regularly. When I had to write it, then it would be the only thing to do and there would be no choice. Let the pressure build. In the meantime I would write a long story about whatever I knew best.

By this time I had paid the check and gone out and turned to the right and crossed the rue de Rennes so that I would not go to the Deux-Magots for coffee and was walking up the rue Bonaparte on the shortest way home.

What did I know best that I had not written about and lost? What did I know about truly and care for the most? There was no choice at all. There was only the choice of streets to take you back fastest to where you worked. I went up Bonaparte to Guynemer, then to the rue d'Assas, across the rue Notre-Dame-des-Champs to the Closerie des Lilas.

I sat in a corner with the afternoon light coming in over my shoulder and wrote in the notebook. The waiter brought me a *café crème* and I drank half of it when it cooled and left it on the table while I wrote. When I stopped writing I did not want to leave the river where I could see the trout in the pool, its surface pushing and swelling smooth against the resistance of the log-driven piles of the bridge. The story was about coming back from the war but there was no mention of the war in it.

But in the morning the river would be there and I must make it and the country and all that would happen. There were days ahead to be doing that each day. No other thing mattered. In my pocket was the money from Germany so there was no problem. When that was gone some other money would come in.

All I must do now was stay sound and good in my head until morning when I would start to work again. In those days we never thought that any of that could be difficult.

9

Ford Maddox Ford
and the Devil's Disciple

The Closerie des Lilas was the nearest good café when we lived down the rue Notre-Dame-des-Champs in the top floor of the pavilion in the courtyard with the sawmill, and it was one of the nicest cafés in Paris. It was warm inside in the winter and in the spring and fall it was very fine outside with the tables under the shade of the trees on the side where the statue of Marshal Ney was, and the square, regular tables under the big awnings along the boulevard. Two of the waiters were our good friends. People from the Dôme and the Rotonde never came to the Lilas. There was no one there they knew, and no one would have stared at them if they came. In those days many people went to the cafés at the corner of the Boulevard Montparnasse and the Boulevard Raspail to be seen publicly and in a way such places anticipated the columnists as the daily substitutes for immortality.

The Closerie des Lilas had once been a café where poets met more or less regularly and the last principal poet had been Paul Fort whom I had never read. But the only poet I ever saw there was Blaise Cendrars, with his broken boxer's face and his pinned-up empty sleeve, rolling a cigarette with his one good hand. He was a good companion until he drank too much and, at that time, when he was lying, he was more interesting than many men telling a story truly. But he was the only poet who came to the Lilas then and I only saw him there once. Most of the clients knew each other only to nod and there were elderly bearded men in well worn clothes who came with their wives or their mistresses and wore or did not wear thin red Legion of Honor ribbons in their lapels. We thought of them all hopefully as scientists or *savants* and they sat almost as long over an aperitif as the men in shabbier clothes who sat with their wives or mistresses over a *café crème* and wore the purple ribbon of the Palms of the Academy, which had nothing to do with the French Academy, and meant, we thought, that they were professors or instructors.

These people made it a comfortable café since they were all interested in each other and in their drinks or coffees, or infusions, and in the papers and periodicals which were fastened to rods, and no one was on exhibition.

There were other people too who lived in the quarter and came to the Lilas, and some of them wore Croix de Guerre ribbons in their lapels and others also had the yellow and green of the Médaille Militaire, and I watched to notice how well they were overcoming the handicap of the loss of limbs, or at the quality of their artificial eyes and the degree of skill with which their faces had been reconstructed. There was always an almost iridescent shiny cast about the considerably reconstructed face, rather like that of a well packed ski run, and we respected these clients more than we did the *savants* or the professors, although the latter might well have done their military service too without experiencing mutilation.

In those days we did not trust anyone who had not been in the war, but we did not completely trust anyone, and there was a strong feeling that Cendrars, our only poet, might well be a little less flashy about his vanished arm. I was glad he had been in the Lilas early in the afternoon before the regular clients had arrived.

On this evening I was sitting at a table outside of the Lilas watching the light change on the trees and the buildings and the passage of the great slow horses of the outer boulevards. The door of the café opened behind me and to my right, and a man came out and walked to my table.

"Oh here you are," he said.

It was Ford Madox Ford, as he called himself then, and he was breathing heavily through a heavy, stained mustache and holding himself as upright as an ambulatory, well clothed, up-ended hogshead.

"May I sit with you?" he asked, sitting down, and his eyes which were a washed-out blue under colorless lids and eyebrows looked out at the boulevard.

"I spent good years of my life that those beasts should be slaughtered humanely," he said.

"You told me," I said.

"I don't think so."

"I'm quite sure."

"Very odd. I've never told anyone in my life."

"Will you have a drink?"

The waiter stood there and Ford told him he would have a Chambéry Cassis. The waiter, who was tall and thin and bald on the top of his head with hair slicked over and who wore a heavy old-style dragoon mustache, repeated the order.

"No. Make it a *fine à l'eau*," Ford said.

"A *fine à l'eau* for Monsieur," the waiter confirmed the order.

I had always avoided looking at Ford when I could and I always held my breath when I was near him in a closed room, but this was the open air and the fallen leaves blew along the sidewalks from my side of the table past his, so I took a good look at him, repented, and looked across the boulevard. The light was changed again and I had missed the change. I took a drink to see if his coming had fouled it, but it still tasted good.

"You're very glum," he said.

"No."

"Yes you are. You need to get out more. I stopped by to ask you to the little evenings we're giving in that amusing Bal Musette near the Place Contrescarpe on the rue Cardinal Lemoine."

"I lived above it for two years before you came to Paris this last time."

"How odd. Are you sure?"

"Yes," I said. "I'm sure. The man who owned it had a taxi and when I had to get a plane he'd take me out to the field, and we'd stop at the zinc bar of the Bal and drink a glass of white wine in the dark before we'd start for the airfield."

"I've never cared for flying," Ford said. "You and your wife plan to come to the Bal Musette Saturday night. It's quite gay. I'll draw you a map so you can find it. I stumbled on it quite by chance."

"It's under 74 rue Cardinal Lemoine," I said. "I lived on the third floor."

"There's no number," Ford said. "But you'll be able to find it if you can find the Place Contrescarpe."

I took another long drink. The waiter had brought Ford's drink and Ford was correcting him. "It wasn't a brandy and soda," he said helpfully but severely. "I ordered a Chambéry vermouth and Cassis."

"It's all right, Jean," I said. "I'll take the *fine*. Bring Monsieur what he orders now."

"What I ordered," corrected Ford.

At that moment a rather gaunt man wearing a cape passed on the sidewalk. He was with a tall woman and he glanced at our table and then away and went on his way down the boulevard.

"Did you see me cut him?" Ford said. "*Did* you see me cut him?"

"No. Who did you cut?"

"Belloc," Ford said. "*Did* I cut him."

"I didn't see it," I said. "Why did you cut him?"

"For every good reason in the world," Ford said. "*Did* I cut him though."

He was thoroughly and completely happy. I had never seen Belloc and I did not believe he had seen us. He looked like a man who had been thinking of something and had glanced at the table almost automatically. I felt badly that Ford had been rude to him, as, being a young man who was commencing his education, I had a high regard for him as an older writer. This is not understandable now but in those days it was a common occurrence.

I thought it would have been pleasant if Belloc had stopped at the table and I might have met him. The afternoon had been spoiled by seeing Ford but I thought Belloc might have made it better.

"What are you drinking brandy for?" Ford asked me. "Don't you know it's fatal for a young writer to start drinking brandy?"

"I don't drink it very often," I said. I was trying to remember what Ezra Pound had told me about Ford, that I must never be rude to him, that I must remember that he only lied when he was very tired, that he was really a good writer and that he had been through very bad domestic troubles. I tried hard to think of these things but the heavy, wheezing, ignoble presence of Ford himself, only touching-distance away, made it difficult. But I tried.

"Tell me why one cuts people," I asked. Until then I had

thought it was something only done in novels by Ouida. I had never been able to read a novel by Ouida, not even at some skiing place in Switzerland where reading matter had run out when the wet south wind had come and there were only the left-behind Tauchnitz editions of before the war. But I was sure, by some sixth sense, that people cut one another in her novels.

"A gentleman," Ford explained, "will always cut a cad."

I took a quick drink of the brandy.

"Would he cut a bounder?" I asked.

"It would be impossible for a gentleman to have known a bounder."

"Then you can only cut someone you have known on terms of equality?" I pursued.

"Naturally."

"How would one ever meet a cad?"

"You might not know it, or the fellow could have become a cad."

"What is a cad?" I asked. "Isn't he someone that one has to thrash within an inch of his life?"

"Not necessarily," Ford said.

"Is Ezra a gentleman?" I asked.

"Of course not," Ford said. "He's an American."

"Can't an American be a gentleman?"

"Perhaps John Quinn," Ford explained. "Certain of your ambassadors."

"Myron T. Herrick?"

"Possibly."

"Was Henry James a gentleman?"

"Very nearly."

"Are you a gentleman?"

"Naturally. I have held His Majesty's commission."

"It's very complicated," I said. "Am I a gentleman?"

"Absolutely not," Ford said.

"Then why are you drinking with me?"

"I'm drinking with you as a promising young writer. As a fellow writer in fact."

"Good of you," I said.

"You might be considered a gentleman in Italy," Ford said magnanimously.

"But I'm not a cad?"

"Of course not, dear boy. Who ever said such a thing?"

"I might become one," I said sadly. "Drinking brandy and all. That was what did it for Lord Harry Hotspur in Trollope. Tell me, was Trollope a gentleman?"

"Of course not."

"You're sure?"

"There might be two opinions. But not in mine."

"Was Fielding? He was a judge."

"Technically perhaps."

"Marlowe?"

"Of course not."

"John Donne?"

"He was a parson."

"It's fascinating," I said.

"I'm glad you're interested," Ford said. "I'll have a brandy and water with you before you go."

After Ford left it was dark and I walked over to the *kiosque* and bought a *Paris-Sport Complet*, the final edition of the afternoon racing paper with the results at Auteuil, and the line on the next day's meeting at Enghien. The waiter Emile, who had replaced Jean on duty, came to the table to see the results of the last race at Auteuil. A great friend of mine who rarely came to the Lilas came over to the table and sat down, and just then as my friend was ordering a drink from Emile the gaunt man in the cape with the tall woman passed us on the sidewalk. His glance drifted toward the table and then away.

"That's Hilaire Belloc," I said to my friend. "Ford was here this afternoon and cut him dead."

"Don't be a silly ass," my friend said. "That's Alestair Crowley, the diabolist. He's supposed to be the wickedest man in the world."

"Sorry," I said.

10

With Pascin at the Dôme

It was a lovely evening and I had worked hard all day and left the flat where we lived over the sawmill at 113 rue Notre-Dame-des-Champs, and walked out through the courtyard with the stacked lumber, closed the door, crossed the street and went into the back door of the bakery that fronted on the Boulevard Montparnasse and out through the good bread smells of the ovens and the shop to the street. The lights were on in the bakery and outside it was the end of the day and I walked in the early dusk up the street and stopped outside the terrace of the Nègre de Toulouse restaurant where our red and white checkered napkins were in the wooden napkin rings in the napkin rack waiting for us to come to dinner. I read the menu mimeographed in purple ink and saw that the *plat du jour* was cassoulet. It made me hungry to read the name.

Mr. Lavigne, the proprietor, asked me how my work had gone and I said it had gone very well. He said he had seen me working on the terrace of the Closerie des Lilas early in the morning but he had not spoken to me because I was so occupied.

"You had the air of a man alone in the jungle," he said.

"I am like a blind pig when I work."

"But were you not in the jungle, Monsieur?"

"In the bush," I said.

I went on up the street looking in the windows and happy

with the spring evening and the people coming past. In the three principal cafés I saw people that I knew by sight and others that I knew to speak to. But there were always much nicer-looking people that I did not know that, in the evening with the lights just coming on, were hurrying to some place to drink together, to eat together and then to make love. The people in the principal cafés might do the same thing or they might just sit and drink and talk and love to be seen by others. The people that I liked and had not met went to the big cafés because they were lost in them and no one noticed them and they could be alone in them and be together. The big cafés were cheap then too, and all had good beer and the apéritifs cost reasonable prices that were clearly marked on the saucers that were served with them.

On this evening I was thinking these wholesome unoriginal thoughts and feeling extraordinarily virtuous because I had worked well and hard on a day when I had wanted to go out to the races very badly. It was necessary to give up going racing in the time of our real poverty and I was still too close to that poverty to risk any money. By any standards we were still very poor and I still made such small economies as saying that I had been asked out for lunch and then spending two hours walking in the Luxembourg gardens and coming back to describe the marvelous lunch to my wife. When you are twenty-five and are a natural heavyweight, missing a meal completely makes you very hungry. But it also sharpens all of your perceptions, and I found that many of the people I wrote about had very strong appetites and a great taste and desire for food, and most of them were looking forward to having a drink.

At the Nègre de Toulouse we drank the good Cahors wine from the quarter, the half, or the full carafe, usually diluting it about one-third with water. At home, over the sawmill, we all of the sadness of the city came suddenly with the first cold rains of winter and there were no more tops to the high white houses as you walked but only the wet blackness of the street and the closed doors of the small shops, the herb sellers, the stationery and the newspaper shops, the mid-wife—second class—and the hotel where Verlaine had died where you had a room on the top floor where you worked.

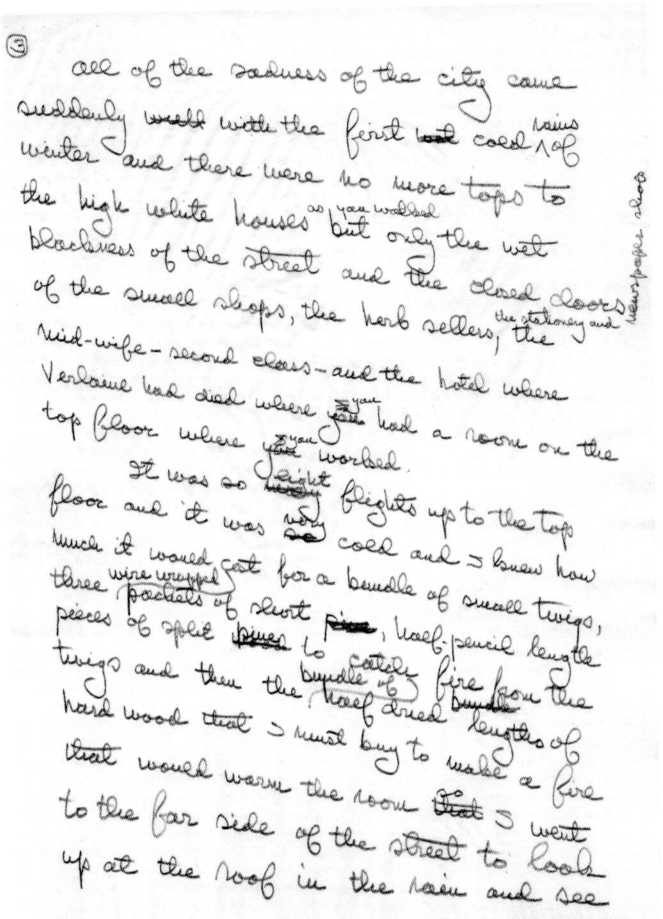

It was so eight flights up to the top floor and it was very cold and I knew how much it would cost for a bundle of small twigs, three wire wrapped packets of short pieces of split pine, half-pencil length pieces of split twigs and then the bundle of fire from the half dried lengths of hard wood that I must buy to make a fire that would warm the room that I went to the far side of the street to look up at the roof in the rain and see

Fig. 1. A handwritten manuscript page from chapter 1, "A Good Café on the Place St.-Michel." In two places Hemingway has crossed out "you" and replaced it with "I" and then returned to "you." Ernest Hemingway Collection, Manuscripts, *A Moveable Feast*, Item 128, p. 3, at the John F. Kennedy Presidential Library and Museum, Boston, MA.

③

drawer of the table and put any mandarines that were left in my pocket. They would freeze if they were left in the room at night

It was wonderful to walk down the long flights of stairs knowing that I had had good luck working. I always worked until I had something done and I always stopped when I knew what was going to happen next. That way I could be sure of going on the next day. But sometimes when I was starting a new story and I could not get it going I would sit in front of the fire and squeeze the peel of the little oranges into the fire edge of the flame and watch the sputter of blue that they made. I would stand and look out over the roofs of Paris and think, do not worry. You have always written before and you will write now. All you have to do is write one true sentence. So I would finally write the truest sentence that I all know So finally I would write one true sentence and then go on from there. It was easy then because there was always one true sentence that you knew or had seen or ~~remembered~~ had heard someone say. If I started to write elaborately, or like some one introducing or presenting something I found that I could cut that scroll work or ornament out and ~~brought~~ throw it away and start with the first true simple declarative sentence I had written. Up in that room I decided that I would write one story about ~~every~~ each thing that I knew about. I was trying to do this all the time I was writing and it was very good and severe discipline. It was in that room too that I learned not to think about anything that I was writing from the time I stopped writing until I started again the next day. That way my subconscious would be working on it and at the same time I would be listening to other people, noticing everything I hoped, learning, I hoped, and I ~~learned~~

The Man who was Marked For Death.
—11—

The afternoon I met Ernest Walsh, the poet, in Ezra's studio he was with two girls in long mink coats and there was a long shiny hired car from Claridges outside in the street with a uniformed chauffeur. The girls were blondes and they had crossed on the same ship with Walsh. The ship had arrived two days before and he had brought them with him to visit Ezra.

Ernest Walsh was dark, intense, poetic and clearly marked for death as a character is marked for death in a motion picture. He was talking to Ezra and I talked with the girls who asked me if I had read her Walsh's poems. I had not and one of them brought out a green covered copy of Harriet Monroe's Poetry: A Magazine of Verse and showed me poems by Walsh in it.

"He gets twelve hundred dollars apiece" she said.

Fig. 4. A handwritten manuscript page from chapter 13, "The Man Who Was Marked for Death." Ernest Hemingway Collection, Manuscripts, *A Moveable Feast,* Item 165, p. 1, at the John F. Kennedy Presidential Library and Museum, Boston, MA.

(15) The winter of the avalanches was like a happy winter in the same again. First we were infiltrated because we had become too confident and careless in our pride. Then it is a tragic and complicated story of the destruction of two people's happiness and the forging of a new happiness in which I should be the last to apportion any blame except my own. But I can remember the magic and the places and the good work that might never have been done without the destruction and how it all ended finally, has nothing to do with this. Dash, any blame was mine to take and possess and understand. But the one who had no guilt ever in anything came well out of it finally and that was one good and lasting thing that came of that year.

[margin, written vertically:] childhood compared to that winter and to the murderous summer that was to follow.

Fig. 5. A handwritten manuscript page of an early draft of "The Pilot Fish and the Rich." Ernest Hemingway Collection, Manuscripts, *A Moveable Feast*, Item 123, p. 15, at the John F. Kennedy Presidential Library and Museum, Boston, MA.

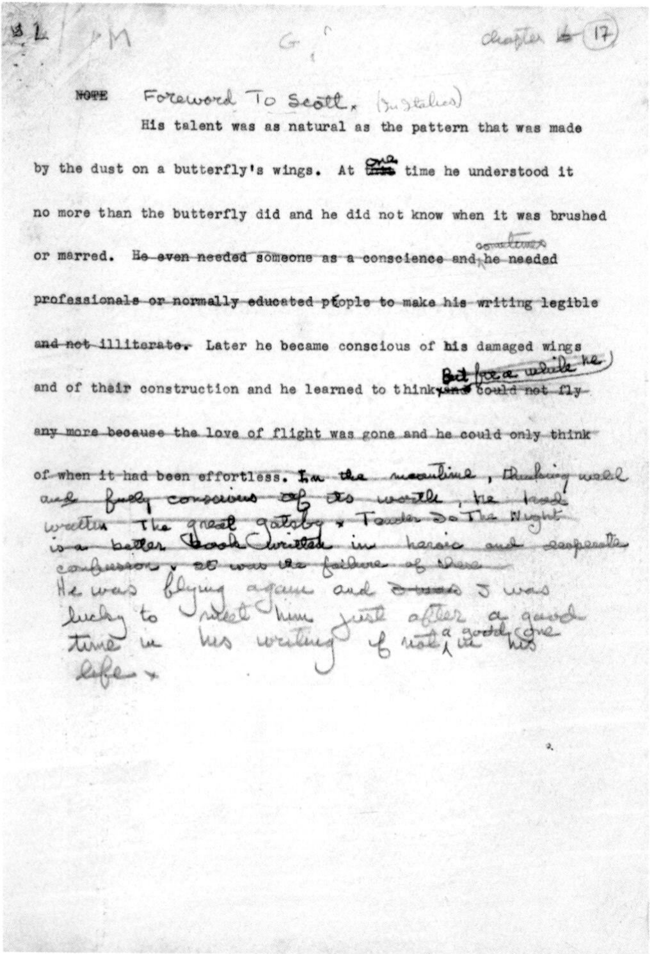

NOTE Foreword To Scott. (in italics)

His talent was as natural as the pattern that was made by the dust on a butterfly's wings. At one time he understood it no more than the butterfly did and he did not know when it was brushed or marred. ~~He even needed someone~~ as a conscience and~~he needed professionals or normally educated people to make his writing legible and not illiterate.~~ Later he became conscious of his damaged wings and of their construction and he learned to think ~~and could not fly any more because the love of flight was gone and he could only think of when it had been effortless.~~

Fig. 6. An early typed draft of the foreword to chapter 17, "Scott Fitzgerald" with handwritten emendations by Hemingway. Ernest Hemingway Collection, Manuscripts, *A Moveable Feast*, Item 172, at the John F. Kennedy Presidential Library and Museum, Boston, MA.

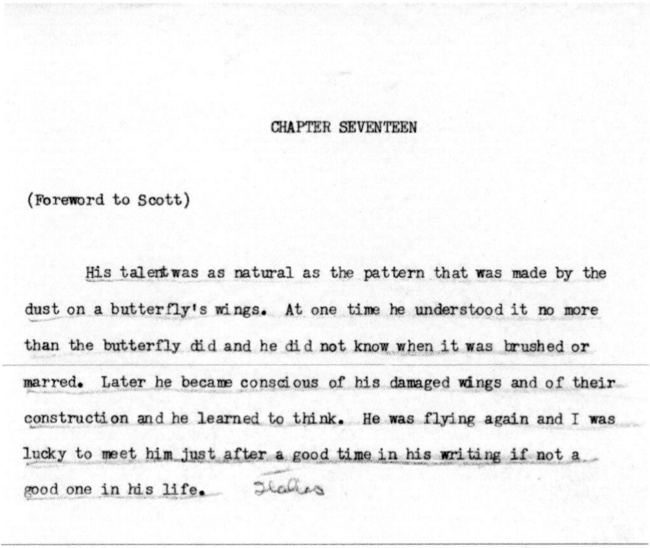

CHAPTER SEVENTEEN

(Foreword to Scott)

His talent was as natural as the pattern that was made by the dust on a butterfly's wings. At one time he understood it no more than the butterfly did and he did not know when it was brushed or marred. Later he became conscious of his damaged wings and of their construction and he learned to think. He was flying again and I was lucky to meet him just after a good time in his writing if not a good one in his life.

Fig. 7. Hemingway's final draft of the foreword to chapter 17, "Scott Fitzgerald." The handwritten annotation is by Hemingway. Ernest Hemingway Collection, Manuscripts, *A Moveable Feast,* Item 188, at the John F. Kennedy Presidential Library and Museum, Boston, MA.

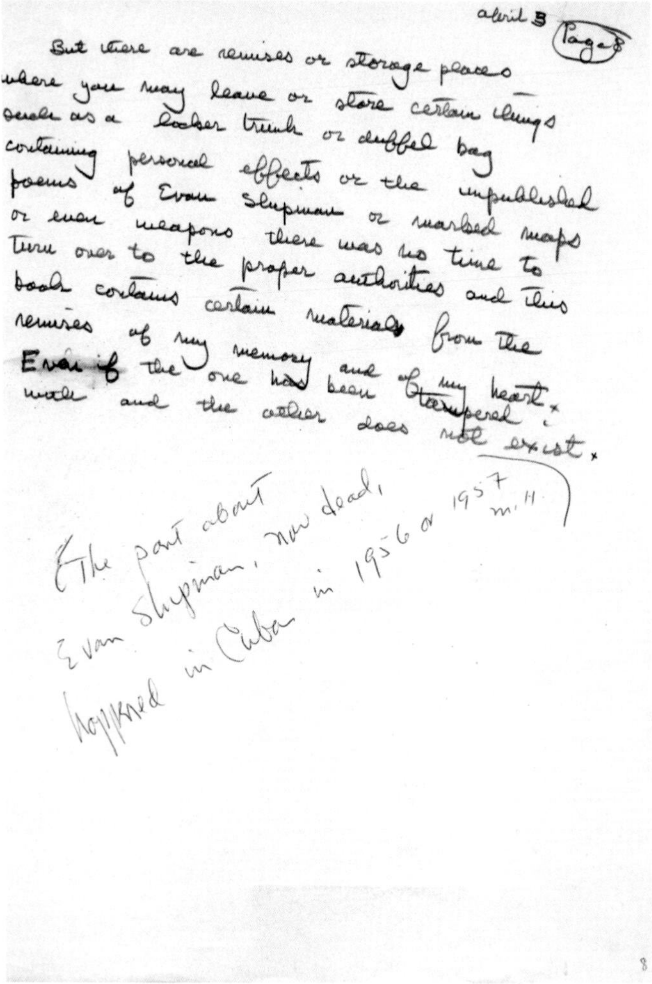

But there are remises or storage places — where you may leave or store certain things such as a locker trunk or duffel bag containing personal effects or the unpublished poems of Evan Shipman or marked maps or even weapons there was no time to turn over to the proper authorities and this book contains certain materials from the remises of my memory and of my heart. Even if the one has been temporal and the other does not exist.

(The part about Evan Shipman, now dead, happened in Cuba in 1956 or 1957. M.H.)

Fig. 8. The final handwritten manuscript page of "*Nada y Pues Nada*" dated April 3 (1961). At the bottom is inscribed by Mary Hemingway: "The part about Evan Shipman, now dead, happened in Cuba in 1956 or 1957. M.H." Ernest Hemingway Collection, Manuscripts, *A Moveable Feast*, Item 124a, p. 8, at the John F. Kennedy Presidential Library and Museum, Boston, MA.

had a Corsican wine that had great authority and a low price. It was a very Corsican wine and you could dilute it by half with water and still receive its message. In Paris, then, you could live very well on almost nothing and by skipping meals occasionally and never buying any new clothes, you could save and have luxuries. But at this time I could not afford to go to the races, even though there was money to be made there if you worked at it. It was before the days of saliva tests and other methods of detecting artificially encouraged horses and doping was very extensively practiced. But handicapping beasts that are receiving stimulants, and detecting the symptoms in the paddock and acting on your perceptions, which sometimes bordered on the extrasensory, then backing them with money you cannot afford to lose, is not the way for a young man supporting a wife and child to get ahead in the full-time job of learning to write prose.

Coming back from The Select now where I had sheered off at the sight of Harold Stearns who I knew would want to talk horses; those animals I was thinking of righteously and lightheartedly as boosted beasts that I had just foresworn at Enghein to work on this day as a serious writer; now full of my evening virtue I passed the collection of inmates of the Rotonde and, scorning vice and the collective instinct, crossed the boulevard to the Dôme. The Dôme was crowded too, but there were people there who had worked.

There were models who had worked and there were painters who had worked until the light was gone and there were writers who had finished a day's work for better or for worse, and there were drinkers and characters, some of whom I knew and some that were only decoration.

I went over and sat with Pascin and two models who were sisters. Pascin had waved to me while I had stood on the sidewalk on the rue Delambre side wondering whether to stop and have a drink or not. Pascin was a very good painter and he was drunk; steady, purposefully drunk and making good sense. The two models were young and pretty. One was very dark, small, beautifully built with a falsely fragile depravity. She was a lesbian who also liked men. The other was child-like and dull but very pretty in a perishable childish way. She was not as well built as her sister, but neither was anyone else that spring.

"The good and the bad sisters," Pascin said. "I have money. What will you drink?"

"*Une demi-blonde,*" I said to the waiter.

"Have a whisky. I have money."

"I like beer."

"If you really liked beer, you'd be at Lipp's. I suppose you've been working."

"Yes."

"It goes?"

"I hope so."

"Good. I'm glad. And everything still tastes good?"

"Yes."

"How old are you?"

"Twenty-five."

"Do you want to bang her?" He looked toward the dark sister and smiled. "She needs it."

"You probably banged her enough today."

She smiled at me with her lips open. "He's wicked," she said. "But he's nice."

"You can take her over to the studio."

"Don't make piggishness," the blonde sister said.

"Who spoke to you?" Pascin asked her.

"Nobody. But I said it."

"Let's be comfortable," Pascin said. "The serious young

writer and the friendly wise old painter and the two beautiful young girls with all of life before them."

We sat there and the girls sipped at their drinks and Pascin drank another *fine à l'eau* and I drank the beer; but no one was comfortable except Pascin. The dark girl was restless and she sat on display turning her profile and letting the light strike the concave planes of her face and showing me her breasts under the hold of the black sweater. Her hair was cropped short and was sleek and dark as an oriental's.

"You've posed all day," Pascin said to her. "Do you have to model that sweater now at the café?"

"It pleases me," she said.

"You look like a Javanese toy," he said.

"Not the eyes," she said. "It's more complicated than that."

"You look like a poor perverted little *poupée*."

"Perhaps," she said. "But alive. That's more than you."

"We'll see about that."

"Good," she said. "I like proofs."

"You didn't have any today?"

"Oh that," she said and turned to catch the last evening light on her face. "You were just excited about your work. He's in love with canvases," she said to me. "There's always some kind of dirtiness."

"You want me to paint you and pay you and bang you to keep my head clear, and be in love with you too," Pascin said. "You poor little doll."

"You like me, don't you, Monsieur?" she asked me.

"Very much."

"But you're too big," she said sadly.

"Everyone is the same size in bed."

"It's not true," her sister said "And I'm tired of this talk."

"Look," Pascin said. "If you think I'm in love with canvases, I'll paint you tomorrow in water colors."

"When do we eat?" her sister asked. "And where?"

"Will you eat with us?" the dark girl asked.

"No. I go to eat with my *légitime*." That was what they said then. Now they say "my *régulière*."

"You have to go?"

"Have to and want to."

"Go on, then," Pascin said. "And don't fall in love with typewriting paper."

"If I do, I'll write with a pencil."

"Water colors tomorrow," he said. "All right, my children, I will drink another and then we eat where you wish."

"Chez Viking," the dark sister said promptly.

"You want to contrast me with all the beautiful Nordic types. No."

"I like it very much at Chez Viking," the dark girl said.

"Me too," her sister urged.

"All right," Pascin agreed. "Good night, *jeune homme*. Sleep well."

"You too."

"They keep me awake," he said. "I never sleep."

"Sleep tonight."

"After Chez Les Vikings?" He grinned with his hat on the back of his head. He looked more like a Broadway character of the Nineties than the lovely painter that he was, and afterwards, when he had hanged himself, I liked to remember him as he was that night at the Dôme. They say the seeds of what we will do are in all of us, but it always seemed to me that in those who make jokes in life the seeds are covered with better soil and with a higher grade of manure.

11

Ezra Pound
and the Measuring Worm

Ezra Pound was always a good friend and he was always doing things for people. The studio where he lived with his wife Dorothy on the rue Notre-Dame-des-Champs was as poor as Gertrude Stein's studio was rich. It had very good light and was heated by a stove and it had paintings by Japanese artists that Ezra knew. They were all noblemen where they came from and wore their hair cut long. Their hair glistened black and swung forward when they bowed and I was very impressed by them but I did not like their paintings. I did not understand them but they did not have any mystery, and when I understood them they meant nothing to me. I was sorry about this but there was nothing I could do about it.

Dorothy's paintings I liked very much and I thought Dorothy was very beautiful and built wonderfully. I also liked the head of Ezra by Gaudier-Brzeska and I liked all of the photographs of this sculptor's work that Ezra showed me and that were in Ezra's book about him. Ezra also liked Picabia's painting but I thought then that it was worthless. I also disliked Wyndham Lewis's painting which Ezra liked very much. He liked the works of his friends, which is beautiful as loyalty but can be disastrous as judgment. We never argued about these things because I kept my mouth shut about things I did not like. If a man liked his friends' painting or writing, I thought it was probably like those people who like their families, and it was not polite to criticize them. Sometimes you can go quite a long time before you criticize families, your own or those by marriage, but it is easier with bad painters because they do not do terrible things and make intimate harm as families can do. With bad painters all you need to do is not look at them. But even when you have learned not to look at families nor listen to them and have learned not to answer letters, families have many ways of being dangerous. Ezra was kinder and more Christian about people than I was. His own writing, when he would hit it right, was so perfect, and he was so sincere in his mistakes and so enamored of his errors, and so kind to people that I always thought of him as a sort of saint. He was also irascible but so, I believe, have been many saints.

Ezra wanted me to teach him to box and it was while we were sparring late one afternoon in his studio that I first met Wyndham Lewis. Ezra had not been boxing very long and I was embarrassed at having him work in front of anyone he knew, and I tried to make him look as good as possible. But it was not very good because he knew how to fence and I was still working to make his left into his fencing hand and move his left foot forward always and bring his right foot up parallel with it. It was just basic moves. I was never able to teach him to throw a left hook and to teach him to shorten his right was something for the future.

Wyndham Lewis wore a wide black hat, like a character in the quarter, and was dressed like someone out of *La Bohème*. He had a face that reminded me of a frog, not a bullfrog but just any frog, and Paris was too big a puddle for him. At that time we believed that any writer or painter could wear any clothes he owned and there was no official uniform for the artist; but Lewis wore the uniform of a prewar artist. It was embarrassing to see him and he watched superciliously while I slipped Ezra's left leads or blocked them with an open right glove.

I wanted us to stop but Lewis insisted we go on, and I could see that, knowing nothing about what was going on, he was waiting, hoping to see Ezra hurt. Nothing happened. I never countered but kept Ezra moving after me sticking out his left hand and throwing a few right hands and then said we were through and washed down with a pitcher of water and toweled off and put on my sweatshirt.

We had a drink of something and I listened while Ezra and Lewis talked about people in London and Paris. I watched Lewis carefully without seeming to look at him, as you do when you are boxing, and I do not think I had ever seen a nastier-looking man. Some people show evil as a great race-horse shows breeding. They have the dignity of a hard *chancre*. Lewis did not show evil; he just looked nasty.

Walking home I tried to think what he reminded me of and there were various things. They were all medical except toe-jam and that was a slang word. I tried to break his face down and describe it but I could only get the eyes. Under the black hat, when I had first seen them, the eyes had been those of an unsuccessful rapist.

"I met the nastiest man I've ever seen today," I told my wife.

"Tatie, don't tell me about him," she said. "Please don't tell me about him. We're just going to have dinner."

About a week afterwards I met Miss Stein and told her I'd met Wyndham Lewis and asked her if she had ever met him.

"I call him 'the Measuring Worm,'" she said. "He comes over from London and he sees a good picture and takes a pencil out of his pocket and you watch him measuring it on the pencil with his thumb. Sighting on it and measuring it and seeing exactly how it is done. Then he goes back to London and does it and it doesn't come out right. He's missed what it's all about."

So I thought of him as the Measuring Worm. It was a kinder and more Christian term than what I had thought about him myself. Later I tried to like him and to be friends with him as I did with nearly all of Ezra's friends when he explained them to me. But this was how he seemed to me on the first day I ever met him in Ezra's studio.

12

A Strange Enough Ending

The way it ended with Gertrude Stein was strange enough. We had become very good friends and I had done a number of practical things for her such as getting her long book started as a serial with Ford and helping type the manuscript and reading her proof and we were getting to be better friends than I could ever wish to be. There is not much future in men being friends with great women although it can be pleasant enough before it gets better or worse, and there is usually even less future with truly ambitious women writers. One time when I gave the excuse for not having stopped in at 27 rue de Fleurus for some time that I did not know whether Miss Stein would be at home, she said, "But Hemingway, you have the run of the place. Don't you know that? I mean it truly. Come in any time and the maidservant"—she used her name but I have forgotten it—"will look after you and you must make yourself at home until I come."

I did not abuse this but sometimes I would stop in and the maidservant would give me a drink and I would look at the pictures and if Miss Stein did not turn up I would thank the maidservant and leave a message and go away. Miss Stein and a companion were getting ready to go south in Miss Stein's car and on this day Miss Stein had asked me to come by in the forenoon to say good-bye. She had asked me to come and visit, Hadley and I staying at an hotel, before and after this trip and we had written many letters. But

Hadley and I had other plans and other places where we wanted to go. Naturally you say nothing about this, but you can still hope to go and then it is impossible. It was something that we never learned. You should know a little about the system of not visiting people. You had to learn it. Much later Picasso told me that he always promised the rich to come when they asked him because it made them so happy and then something would happen and he would be unable to appear. But that had nothing to do with Miss Stein and he said it about other people.

It was a lovely spring day and I walked down from the Place de l'Observatoire through the little Luxembourg. The horse-chestnut trees were in blossom and there were many children playing on the graveled walks with their nurses sitting on the benches, and I saw wood pigeons in the trees and heard others that I could not see.

The maidservant opened the door before I rang and told me to come in and to wait. Miss Stein would be down at any moment. It was before noon but the maidservant poured me a glass of *eau-de-vie,* put it in my hand and winked happily. The colorless alcohol felt good on my tongue and it was still in my mouth when I heard someone speaking to Miss Stein as I had never heard one person speak to another; never, anywhere, ever.

Then Miss Stein's voice came pleading and begging, saying, "Don't, pussy. Don't. Don't, please don't. I'll do anything, pussy, but please don't do it. Please don't. Please don't, pussy."

I swallowed the drink and put the glass down on the table and started for the door. The maidservant shook her finger at me and whispered, "Don't go. She'll be right down."

"I have to go," I said and tried not to hear any more as I left but it was still going on and the only way I could not hear it was to be gone. It was bad to hear and the answers were worse.

In the courtyard I said to the maidservant, "Please say I came to the courtyard and met you. That I could not wait because a friend is sick. Say *bon voyage* for me. I will write."

"*C'est entendu,* Monsieur. What a shame you cannot wait."

"Yes," I said. "What a shame."

That was the way it finished for me, stupidly enough, although I still did the small jobs, made the necessary appearances, brought people that were asked for and waited dismissal with most of the other men friends when that epoch came and the new friends moved in. It was sad to see new worthless pictures hung in with the great pictures but it made no difference any more. Not to me it didn't. She quarreled with nearly all of us that were fond of her except Juan Gris and she couldn't quarrel with him because he was dead. I am not sure that he would have cared because he was past caring and it showed in his paintings.

Finally she even quarreled with the new friends but none of us followed it any more. She got to look like a Roman emperor and that was fine if you liked your women to look like Roman emperors. But Picasso had painted her, and I could remember her, when she looked like a woman from Friuli.

In the end everyone, or not quite everyone, made friends again in order not to be stuffy or righteous. I did too. But I could never make friends again truly, neither in my heart nor in my head. When you cannot make friends any more in your head is the worst. It never occurred to me until many years later that anyone could hate anyone because they had learned to write conversation from that novel that started off with the quotation from the garage keeper. But it was really much more complicated than that.

The Man Who Was Marked for Death

The afternoon I met Ernest Walsh, the poet, in Ezra's studio, he was with two girls in long mink coats and there was a long, shiny, hired car from Claridge's outside in the street with a uniformed chauffeur. The girls were blondes and they had crossed on the same ship with Walsh. The ship had arrived the day before and he had brought them with him to visit Ezra.

Ernest Walsh was dark, intense, faultlessly Irish, poetic and clearly marked for death as a character is marked for death in a motion picture. He was talking to Ezra and I talked with the girls who asked me if I had read Mr. Walsh's poems. I had not and one of them brought out a green-covered copy of Harriet Monroe's *Poetry, A Magazine of Verse* and showed me poems by Walsh in it.

"He gets twelve hundred dollars apiece," she said.

"For each poem," the other girl said.

My recollection was that I received twelve dollars a page, if that, from the same magazine. "He must be a very great poet," I said.

"It's more than Eddie Guest gets," the first girl told me.

"It's more than who's that other poet gets. You know."

"Kipling," her friend said.

"It's more than anybody gets ever," the first girl said.

"Are you staying in Paris very long?" I asked them.

"Well no. Not really. We're with a group of friends."

"We came over on this boat, you know. But there wasn't anyone on it really. Mr. Walsh was on it of course."

"Doesn't he play cards?" I asked.

She looked at me in a disappointed but understanding way.

"No. He doesn't have to. Not writing poetry the way he can write it."

"What ship are you going back on?"

"Well that depends. It depends on the boats and on a lot of things. Are you going back?"

"No. I'm getting by all right."

"This is sort of the poor quarter over here, isn't it?"

"Yes. But it's pretty good. I work the cafés and I'm out at the track."

"Can you go out to the track in those clothes?"

"No. This is my café outfit."

"It's kind of cute," one of the girls said. "I'd like to see some of that café life. Wouldn't you, dear?"

"I would," the other girl said. I wrote their names down in my address book and promised to call them at Claridge's. They were nice girls and I said good-bye to them and to Walsh and to Ezra. Walsh was still talking to Ezra with great intensity.

"Don't forget," the taller one of the girls said.

"How could I?" I told her and shook hands with them both again.

The next I heard from Ezra about Walsh was that he had been bailed out of Claridge's by some lady admirers of poetry and of young poets who were marked for death, and the next thing, some time after that, was that he had financial backing from another source and was going to start a new magazine in the quarter as a co-editor.

At the time the *Dial,* an American literary magazine edited by Scofield Thayer, gave an annual award of, I believe, a thousand dollars for excellence in the practice of letters by a contributor. This was a huge sum for any straight writer to receive in those days, in addition to the prestige, and the award had gone to various people, all deserving, naturally. Two people, then, could live comfortably and well in Europe on five dollars a day and could travel. The advance I had received from an American publisher on my first full-length book of short stories was two hundred dollars and supplemented by loans and savings it meant a winter to ski and write in the Vorarlberg.

This Quarter, of which Walsh was one of the editors, was alleged to be going to award a very substantial sum to the contributor whose work should be judged the best at the end of the first four issues.

If the news was passed around by gossip or rumor, or if it was a matter of personal confidence, cannot be said. Let us hope and believe always that it was completely honorable in every way. Certainly nothing could ever be said or imputed against Walsh's co-editor ever.

It was not long after I heard rumors of this alleged award that Walsh asked me to lunch one day at a restaurant that was the best and the most expensive in the Boulevard St.-Michel quarter and after the oysters, expensive flat faintly coppery *marennes,* not the familiar, deep, inexpensive *portugaises,* and a bottle of Pouilly-Fuissé, began to lead up to it delicately. He appeared to be conning me as he had conned the shills from the boat—if they were shills and if he had conned them, of course—and when he asked me if I would like another dozen of the flat oysters as he called them, I said I would like them very much. He did not bother to look marked for death with me and this was a relief. He knew I knew he had the con, not the kind you con with but the kind you died of then and how bad it was, and he did not bother to have to cough, and I was grateful for this at the table. I was wondering if he ate the flat oysters in the same way the whores in Kansas City, who were marked for death and practically everything else, always wished to swallow semen as a sovereign remedy against the con; but I did not ask him. I began my second dozen of the flat oysters, picking them from their bed of crushed ice on the silver plate, watching their unbelievably delicate brown edges react and cringe as I squeezed lemon juice on them and separated the holding muscle from the shell and lifted them to chew them carefully.

"Ezra's a great, great poet," Walsh said, looking at me with his own dark poet's eyes.

"Yes," I said. "And a fine man."

"Noble," Walsh said. "Truly noble." We ate and drank in silence as a tribute to Ezra's nobility. I missed Ezra and wished he were there. He could not afford *marennes* either.

"Joyce is great," Walsh said. "Great. Great."

"Great," I said. "And a good friend." We had become friends in his wonderful period after the finishing of *Ulysses* and before starting what was called for a long time *Work in Progress*. I thought of Joyce and remembered many things.

"I wish his eyes were better," Walsh said.

"So does he," I said.

"It is the tragedy of our time," Walsh told me.

"Everybody has something wrong with them," I said, trying to cheer up the lunch.

"You haven't." He gave me all his charm and more, and then he marked himself for death.

"You mean I am not marked for death?" I asked. I could not help it.

"No. You're marked for Life." He capitalized the word.

"Give me time," I said.

He wanted a good steak, rare, and I ordered two tourne-dos with sauce Béarnaise. I figured the butter would be good for him.

"What about a red wine?" he asked. The *sommelier* came and I ordered a Châteauneuf du Pape. I would walk it off afterwards along the quais. He could sleep it off, or do what he wanted to. I might take mine someplace, I thought.

It came as we finished the steak and french-fried potatoes and were two-thirds through the Châteauneuf du Pape which is not a luncheon wine.

"There's no use beating around the bush," he said. "You know you're to get the award, don't you?"

"Am I?" I said. "Why?"

"You're to get it," he said. He started to talk about my writing and I stopped listening. I was embarrassed and it made me feel sick for people to talk about my writing to my face, and I looked at him and his marked-for-death look and I thought, you con man conning me with your con. I've seen a battalion in the dust on the road, a third of them for death or worse and no special marks on them, the dust was for all, and you and your marked for death look, you con man, making a living out of your death. Now you will con me. Con not, lest thou be not conned. Death was not conning with him. It was coming all right.

"I don't think I deserve it, Ernest," I said, enjoying using my own name, that I hated, to him. "Besides, Ernest, it would not be ethical, Ernest."

"It's strange we have the same name, isn't it?"

"Yes, Ernest," I said. "It's a name we must both live up to. You see what I mean, don't you, Ernest?"

"Yes, Ernest," he said. He gave me complete, sad Irish understanding and the charm.

So I was always very nice to him and to his magazine and when he had his hemorrhages and left Paris asking me to see his magazine through the printers who did not read English, I did that. I had seen one of the hemorrhages, it was very legitimate, and I knew that he would die all right, and it pleased me at that time, which was a difficult time in my life, to be extremely nice to him, as it pleased me to call him Ernest. Also, I liked and admired his co-editor. She had not promised me any award. She only wished to build a good magazine and pay her contributors well.

One day, years later, I met Joyce who was walking along the Boulevard St.-Germain after having been to a matinee alone. He liked to listen to the actors, although he could not see them. He asked me to have a drink with him and we went to the Deux-Magots and ordered dry sherry although you will always read that he drank only Swiss white wine.

"Now about Walsh," Joyce said.

"A such and such alive is a such and such dead," I said.

"Did he promise you that award?" Joyce asked.

"Yes."

"I thought so," Joyce said.

"Did he promise it to you?"

"Yes," Joyce said. After a time he asked, "Do you think he promised it to Pound?"

"I don't know."

"Best not to ask him," Joyce said. We left it at that. I cannot remember when Walsh died. It was long before that evening with Joyce. But I can remember telling Joyce of my first meeting with him in Ezra's studio with the girls in the long fur coats and how very happy it made him to hear the story.

14

Evan Shipman at the Lilas

From the day I had found Sylvia Beach's library I had read all of Turgenev, what had been published in English of Gogol, the Constance Garnett translations of Tolstoi and the English translations of Chekov. In Toronto, before we had ever come to Paris, I had been told Katherine Mansfield was a good short-story writer, even a great short-story writer, but trying to read her after Chekov was like hearing the carefully artificial tales of a young old-maid compared to those of an articulate and knowing physician who was a good and simple writer. Mansfield was like near-beer. It was better to drink water. But Chekov was not water except for the clarity. There were some stories that seemed to be only journalism. But there were wonderful ones too.

In Dostoyevsky there were things believable and not to be believed, but some so true they changed you as you read them; frailty and madness, wickedness and saintliness, and the insanity of gambling were there to know as you knew the landscape and the roads in Turgenev, and the movement of troops, the terrain and the officers and the men and the fighting in Tolstoi. Tolstoi made the writing of Stephen Crane on the Civil War seem like the brilliant imagining of a sick boy who had never seen war but had only read the battles and chronicles and seen the Brady photographs that I had read and seen at my grandparents' house. Until I read the *Chartreuse de Parme* by Stendhal I had never read of war as it was except in Tolstoi, and the wonderful Waterloo account by Stendhal was an accidental piece in a book that had much dullness. To have come on all this new world of writing, with time to read in a city like Paris where there was a way of living well and working, no matter how poor you were, was like having a great treasure given to you. You could take your treasure with you when you traveled too, and in the mountains where we lived in Switzerland and Italy, until we found Schruns in the high valley in the Vorarlberg in Austria, there were always the books, so that you lived in the new world you had found, the snow and the forests and the glaciers and their winter problems and your high shelter or your pension in the Hotel Taube in the village at night; and you could live in the other wonderful world the Russian writers were giving you. At first there were the Russians; then there were all the others. But for a long time there were the Russians.

I remember asking Ezra once when we had walked home from playing tennis out on the Boulevard Arago, and he had asked me into his studio for a drink, what he really thought about Dostoyevsky.

"To tell you the truth," Ezra said, "I've never read the Rooshians."

It was a straight answer and Ezra had never given me any other kind verbally, but I felt very bad because here was the man I liked and trusted the most as a critic then, the man who believed in the *mot juste*—the one and only correct word to use—the man who had taught me to distrust adjectives as I would later learn to distrust certain people in certain given situations; and I wanted his opinion on a man who almost never used the *mot juste* and yet had made his people come alive at times, as almost no one else did.

"Keep to the French," Ezra said. "You've plenty to learn there."

"I know it," I said. "I've plenty to learn everywhere."

Later after leaving Ezra's studio and walking along the street to where we now lived in the courtyard of the sawmill, looking down the high-sided street to the opening at the end where the bare trees showed and behind them the far façade of the Bal Bullier across the width of the Boulevard St.-Michel, I opened the gate of the sawmill, went in past the fresh-sawn lumber and left my racket in its press beside the stairs that led to the top floor of the pavillion. I called up the stairs but there was no one home.

"Madame has gone out and the *bonne* and the baby too," the wife of the sawmill owner told me. She was a difficult woman, over-plump, with brassy hair, and I thanked her.

"There was a young man to see you," she said, using the term *jeune homme* instead of monsieur. "He said he would be at the Lilas."

"Thank you very much," I said. "If Madame comes in, please tell her I am at the Lilas."

"She went out with friends," the wife said and gathering her purple dressing gown about her went on high heels into the doorway of her own *domaine* without closing the door.

I walked down the street between the high, stained and streaked white houses and turned to the right at the open, sunny end and went into the sun-striped dusk of the Lilas.

There was no one there I knew and I went outside onto the terrace and found Evan Shipman waiting. He was a fine poet and he knew and cared about horses, writing and painting. He rose and I saw him tall and pale and thin, his white shirt dirty and worn at the collar, his tie carefully knotted, his worn and wrinkled grey suit, his fingers stained darker than his hair, his nails dirty and his loving, deprecatory smile that he held tightly not to show his bad teeth.

"It's good to see you, Hem," he said.

"How are you, Evan?" I asked.

"A little down," he said. "I think I have the 'Mazeppa' licked though. Have you been going well?"

"I hope so," I said. "I was out playing tennis with Ezra when you came by."

"Is Ezra well?"

"Very."

"I'm so glad. Hem, you know I don't think that owner's wife where you live likes me. She wouldn't let me wait upstairs for you."

"I'll tell her," I said.

"Don't bother. I can always wait here. It's very pleasant in the sun now, isn't it?"

"It's fall now," I said. "I don't think you dress warmly enough."

"It's only cool in the evening," Evan said. "I'll wear my coat."

"Do you know where it is?"

"No. But it's somewhere safe."

"How do you know?"

"Because I left the poem in it." He laughed heartily holding his lips tightly over the teeth. "Have a whisky with me, please, Hem."

"All right."

"Jean," Evan got up and called the waiter. "Two whiskies please."

Jean brought the bottle and the glasses and two ten-franc saucers with the syphon. He used no measuring glass and poured the whisky until the glasses were more than three-quarters full. Jean loved Evan who often went out and worked with him at his garden in Montrouge, out beyond the Porte d'Orléans, on Jean's day off.

"You mustn't exaggerate," Evan said to the tall old waiter.

"They are two whiskies, aren't they?" the waiter asked.

We added water and Evan said, "Take the first sip very carefully, Hem. Properly handled, they will hold us for some time."

"Are you taking any care of yourself?" I asked.

"Yes, truly, Hem. Let's talk about something else, should we?"

There was no one sitting on the terrace and the whisky was warming us both although I was better dressed for the fall than Evan as I wore a sweatshirt for underwear and then a shirt and a blue wool French sailor's sweater over the shirt.

"I've been wondering about Dostoyevsky," I said. "How can a man write so badly, so unbelievably badly, and make you feel so deeply?"

"It can't be the translation," Evan said. "She makes the Tolstoi come out well written."

"I know. I remember how many times I tried to read *War and Peace* until I got the Constance Garnett translation."

"They say it can be improved on," Evan said. "I'm sure it can although I don't know Russian. But we both know translators. But it comes out as a hell of a novel, the greatest I suppose, and you can read it over and over."

"I know," I said. "But you can't read Dostoyevsky over and over. I had *Crime and Punishment* on a trip when we ran out of books down at Schruns, and I couldn't read it again when we had nothing to read. I read the Austrian papers and studied German until we found some Trollope in Tauchnitz."

"God bless Tauchnitz," Evan said. The whisky had lost its burning quality and was now, when water was added, simply much too strong.

"Dostoyevsky was a shit, Hem," Evan went on. "He was best on shits and saints. He makes wonderful saints. It's a shame we can't reread him."

"I'm going to try *The Brothers* again. It was probably my fault."

"You can read some of it again. Most of it. But then it will start to make you angry, no matter how great it is."

"Well, we were lucky to have had it to read the first time and maybe there will be a better translation."

"But don't let it tempt you, Hem."

"I won't. I'm trying to do it so it will make it without you knowing it, and so the more you read it, the more there will be."

"Well I'm backing you in Jean's whisky," Evan said.

"He'll get in trouble doing that," I said.

"He's in trouble already," Evan said.

"How?"

"They're changing the management," Evan said. "The new owners want to have a different clientele that will spend some money and they are going to put in an American bar. The waiters are going to be in white jackets, Hem, and they have been ordered to be ready to shave off their mustaches."

"They can't do that to André and Jean."

"They shouldn't be able to, but they will."

"Jean has had a mustache all his life. That's a dragoon's mustache. He served in a cavalry regiment."

"He's going to have to cut it off."

I drank the last of the whisky.

"Another whisky, Monsieur?" Jean asked. "A whisky, Monsieur Shipman?" His drooping mustache was a part of his thin, kind face, and the bald top of his head glistened under the strands of hair that were slicked across it.

"Don't do it, Jean," I said. "Don't take a chance."

"There is no chance," he said, softly to us. "There is much confusion. Many are leaving."

"Don't bring it, Jean."

"*Entendu*, Messieurs," he said aloud. He went into the café and came out carrying the bottle of whisky, two large glasses, two ten-franc gold-rimmed saucers and a seltzer bottle.

"No, Jean," I said.

He put the glasses down on the saucers and filled them almost to the brim with whisky and took the remains of the bottle back into the café. Evan and I squirted a little seltzer into the glasses.

"It was a good thing Dostoyevsky didn't know Jean," Evan said. "He might have died of drink."

"What are we going to do with these?"

"Drink them," Evan said. "It's a protest. It's direct action."

On the following Monday when I went to the Lilas to work in the morning, André served me a *bovril*, which is a cup of beef extract and water. He was short and blond and where his stubby mustache had been, his lip was as bare as a priest's. He was wearing a white American barman's coat.

"And Jean?"

"He won't be in until tomorrow."

"How is he?"

"It took him longer to reconcile himself. He was in a heavy cavalry regiment throughout the war. He had the Croix de Guerre and the Médaille Militaire."

"I did not know he was so badly wounded."

"No. He was wounded of course but it was the other sort of Médaille Militaire he has. For gallantry."

"Tell him I asked for him."

"Of course," André said. "I hope it will not take him too long to reconcile himself."

"Please give him Mr. Shipman's greeting too."

"Mr. Shipman is with him," André said. "They are gardening together."

15

An Agent of Evil

The last thing Ezra said to me before he left the rue Notre-Dame-des-Champs to go to Rapallo was, "Hem, I want you to keep this jar of opium and give it to Dunning only when he needs it."

It was a large cold-cream jar and when I unscrewed the top the content was dark and sticky and it had the smell of very raw opium. Ezra had bought it from an Indian chief, he said, on the avenue de l'Opéra near the Boulevard des Italiens and it had been very expensive. I thought it must have come from the old Hole in the Wall bar which was a hangout for deserters and for dope peddlers during and after the first war. The Hole in the Wall was a narrow bar, almost a passageway, on the rue des Italiens with a red-painted façade, which had, at one time, a rear exit into the sewers of Paris from which you were supposed to be able to reach the catacombs. Dunning was Ralph Cheever Dunning, a poet who smoked opium and forgot to eat. When he was smoking too much he could only drink milk and he wrote in *terza rima* which endeared him to Ezra who also found fine qualities in his poetry. He lived in the same courtyard where Ezra had his studio and Ezra had called me in to help him when Dunning was dying a few weeks before Ezra was to leave Paris.

"Dunning is dying," Ezra's message said. "Please come at once."

Dunning looked like a skeleton as he lay on the mattress

and he would certainly have eventually died of malnutrition but I finally convinced Ezra that few people ever died while speaking in well rounded phrases and that I had never known any man to die while speaking in *terza rima* and that I doubted even if Dante could do it. Ezra said he was not talking in *terza rima* and I said that perhaps it only sounded like *terza rima* because I had been asleep when he had sent for me. Finally after a night with Dunning waiting for death to come, the matter was put in the hands of a physician and Dunning was taken to a private clinic to be disintoxicated. Ezra guaranteed his bills and enlisted the aid of I do not know which lovers of poetry on Dunning's behalf. Only the delivery of the opium in any true emergency was left to me. It was a sacred charge coming from Ezra and I only hoped I could live up to it and determine the state of a true emergency. It came when Ezra's concierge arrived one Sunday morning at the sawmill yard and shouted up to the open window where I was studying the racing form, "*Monsieur Dunning est monté sur le toit et refuse catégoriquement de descendre.*"

Dunning having climbed to the roof of the studio and refusing categorically to come down seemed a valid emergency and I found the opium jar and walked up the street with the concierge who was a small and intense woman who was very excited by the situation.

"Monsieur has what is needed?" she asked me.

"Absolutely," I said. "There will be no difficulty."

"Monsieur Pound thinks of everything," she said. "He is kindness personified."

"He is indeed," I said. "And I miss him every day."

"Let us hope that Monsieur Dunning will be reasonable."

"I have what it takes," I assured her.

When we reached the courtyard where the studios were the concierge said, "He's come down."

"He must have known I was coming," I said.

I climbed the outside stairway that led to Dunning's place and knocked. He opened the door. He was gaunt and seemed unusually tall.

"Ezra asked me to bring you this," I said and handed him the jar. "He said you would know what it was."

He took the jar and looked at it. Then he threw it at me. It struck me on the chest or the shoulder and rolled down the stairs.

"You son of a bitch," he said. "You bastard."

"Ezra said you might need it," I said. He countered that by throwing a milk bottle.

"You are sure you don't need it?" I asked.

He threw another milk bottle. I retreated and he hit me with another milk bottle in the back. Then he shut the door.

I picked up the jar which was only slightly cracked and put it in my pocket.

"He did not seem to want the gift of Monsieur Pound," I said to the concierge.

"Perhaps he will be tranquil now," she said.

"Perhaps he has some of his own," I said.

"Poor Monsieur Dunning," she said.

The lovers of poetry that Ezra had organized rallied to Dunning's aid again eventually. My own intervention and that of the concierge had been unsuccessful. The jar of alleged opium which had been cracked I stored wrapped in waxed paper and carefully tied in one of an old pair of riding boots. When Evan Shipman and I were removing my personal effects from that apartment some years later the boots were still there but the jar was gone. I do not know the date of Dunning's actual death, nor if he ever died, nor why he threw the milk bottles at me unless he remembered my lack of credulity the night of his first dying, or whether it was only an innate dislike of my personality. But I remember the happiness that the phrase "*Monsieur Dunning est monté sur le toit et refuse catégoriquement de descendre*" gave to Evan Shipman. He believed there was something symbolic about it. I would not know. Perhaps Dunning took me for an agent of evil or of the police. I only know that Ezra tried to be kind to Dunning as he was kind to so many people and I always hoped Dunning was as fine a poet as Ezra believed him to be. For a poet he threw a very accurate milk bottle. But Ezra, who was a very great poet, played a good game of tennis too. Evan Shipman, who was a very fine poet and who truly did not care if his poems were ever published, felt that it should remain a mystery.

"We need more true mystery in our lives, Hem," he once said to me. "The completely unambitious writer and the really good unpublished poem are the things we lack most at this time. There is, of course, the problem of sustenance."

I have never seen anything written about Evan Shipman and this part of Paris nor about his unpublished poems and that is why I feel it so important to include him in this book.

16

Winters in Schruns

When there were the three of us instead of just the two, it was the cold and the weather that finally drove us out of Paris in the winter time. Alone there was no problem really when you got used to it. I could always go to a café to write and could work all morning over a *café crème* while the waiters cleaned and swept out the café and it gradually grew warmer. My wife could go to work at the piano in a cold place and with enough sweaters keep warm playing and come home to nurse Bumby. It was wrong to take a baby to a café in the winter though; even a baby that never cried and watched everything that happened and was never bored. There were no baby-sitters then and Bumby would stay happy in his tall cage bed with his big, wonderful cat named F. Puss. There were people who said that it was dangerous to leave a cat with a baby. The most ignorant and prejudiced said that a cat would suck a baby's breath and kill him. Others said that a cat would lie on a baby and the cat's weight would smother him. F. Puss lay beside Bumby in the tall cage bed and watched the door with his big yellow eyes, and would let no one come near him when we were out; and Marie, the *femme de ménage*, had to be away. There was no need for baby-sitters. F. Puss was the baby-sitter.

But when you are really poor, and we were truly poor when I had given up all journalism when we came back from Canada, and could sell no stories at all, it was too rough with a baby in Paris in the winter; even with Mr. Bumby who at three months had crossed the North Atlantic on a twelve-day small Cunarder that sailed from New York via Halifax in January, and never cried once on the trip and laughed happily when he would be barricaded in a bunk so he could not fall out when we were in heavy weather.

We went to Schruns in the Vorarlberg in Austria. After going through Switzerland you came to the Austrian frontier at Feldkirch. The train went through Liechtenstein and stopped at Bludenz where there was a small branch line that ran along a pebbly trout river through a valley of farms and forest to Schruns, which was a sunny market town with sawmills, stores, inns and a good, year-around hotel called the Taube where we lived.

The rooms at the Taube were large and comfortable with big stoves, big windows and big beds with good blankets and feather coverlets. The meals were simple and excellent and the dining room and the wood-planked public bar were well heated and friendly. The valley was wide and open so there was good sun. The pension was about two dollars a day for the three of us, and as the Austrian schilling went down with inflation, our room and food were less all the time. There was no desperate inflation and poverty there as there had been in Germany. The schilling went up and down; but its course was down.

There were no ski lifts from Schruns and no funiculars; but there were logging trails and cattle trails that led up different mountain valleys to the high mountain country. You climbed on foot carrying your skis and higher up, where the snow was too deep, you climbed on seal skins that you attached to the bottoms of the skis. At the tops of mountain valleys there were the big Alpine Club huts for summer climbers where you could sleep and leave payment for any wood you used. In some you had to pack up your own wood, or if you were going on a long tour in the high mountains and the glaciers, you hired someone to pack wood and supplies up with you, and established a base. The most famous of these high base huts were the Lindauer-Hütte, the Madlener-Haus and the Wiesbadener-Hütte.

In back of the Taube Hotel there was a sort of practice slope where you ran through orchards and fields and there was another good slope behind Tschagguns across the valley where there was a beautiful inn with a wonderful collection of chamois horns on the walls of the drinking room. It was from behind the lumber village of Tschagguns, which was on the far edge of the valley, that the good skiing went all the way up until you could eventually cross the mountains and get over the Silvretta into the Klosters area.

Schruns was a wonderful place for Bumby who had a very dark-haired beautiful girl to take him out in the sun in his sleigh and look after him, and Hadley and I had all the new country to learn and the new villages, and the people of the town were very friendly. Herr Walther Lent who was a pioneer high-mountain skier and at one time had been a partner with Hannes Schneider, the great Arlberg skier, making ski waxes for climbing and all snow conditions, was starting a school for Alpine skiing and we both enrolled. Walther Lent's system was to get his pupils off the practice slopes as soon as possible and into the high mountains on trips. Skiing was not the way it is now, the spiral fracture had not become common then, and no one could afford a broken leg. There were no ski patrols. Anything you ran down from, you had to climb up to first, and you could run down only as often as you could climb up. That made you have legs that were fit to run down with.

Walther Lent believed the fun of skiing was to get up into

the highest mountain country where there was no one else and where the snow was untracked and then travel from one high Alpine Club hut to another over the top passes and glaciers of the Alps. You must not have a binding that could break your leg if you fell. The ski should come off before it broke your leg. What he really loved was unroped glacier skiing, but for that we had to wait until spring when the crevasses were sufficiently covered.

Hadley and I had loved skiing since we had first done it together in Switzerland and later at Cortina d'Ampezzo in the Dolomites when Bumby was going to be born and the doctor in Milan had given her permission to continue to ski if I would promise that she would not fall down. This took a very careful selection of terrain and of runs and absolutely controlled running, but she had beautiful, wonderfully strong legs and fine control of her skis, and she did not fall. She would not fall any more than she would have fallen in un-roped glacier skiing. We all knew the different snow conditions and everyone knew how to run in deep powder snow.

We loved the Vorarlberg and we loved Schruns. We would go there about Thanksgiving time and stay until nearly Easter. There was always the skiing although because Schruns was not high enough for a ski resort except in a heavy snowy winter, you had to climb for it. But climbing was fun and no one minded it in those days. You set a certain pace well under the speed at which you could climb, and it was easy and your heart felt good and you were proud of the weight of your rucksack. Part of the climb up to the Madlener-Haus was steep and very tough. But the second time you made that climb it was easier, and finally you made it easily with double the weight you had carried at first.

We were always hungry and every meal time was a great

event. We drank light or dark beer and new wines and wines that were a year old sometimes. The white wines were the best. For other drinks there was wonderful kirsch made in the valley and Enzian *Schnapps* distilled from mountain gentian. Sometimes for dinner there would be jugged hare with a rich red wine sauce, and sometimes venison with chestnut sauce. We would drink red wine with these even though it was more expensive than white wine, and the very best cost twenty cents a liter. Ordinary red wine was much cheaper and we packed it up in kegs to the Madlener-Haus.

We had a store of books that Sylvia Beach had let us take for the winter and we could bowl with the people of the town in the alley that gave onto the summer garden of the hotel. Once or twice a week there was a poker game in the dining room of the hotel with all the windows shuttered and the door locked. Gambling was forbidden in Austria then and I played with Herr Nels, the hotel keeper, Herr Lent of the Alpine ski school, a banker of the town, the public prosecutor and the captain of Gendarmerie. It was a stiff game and they were all good poker players except that Herr Lent played too wildly because the ski school was not making any money. The captain of Gendarmerie would raise his finger to his ear when he would hear the pair of gendarmes stop outside the door when they made their rounds, and we would be silent until they had gone on.

In the cold of the morning as soon as it was light the maid would come into the room and shut the windows and make a fire in the big porcelain stove. Then the room was warm, there was breakfast of fresh bread or toast with delicious fruit preserves and big bowls of coffee, fresh eggs and wonderful ham if you wanted it. There was a dog named Schnauz that slept on the foot of the bed who loved to go on ski trips and to ride on my back or over my shoulder when I ran down hill. He was Mr. Bumby's friend too and would go for walks with him and his nurse beside the small sleigh.

Schruns was a good place to work. I know because I did the most difficult job of rewriting I have ever done there in the winter of 1925 and 1926, when I had to take the first draft of *The Sun Also Rises* which I had written in one sprint of six weeks, and make it into a novel. But I cannot remember what stories I wrote there. There were several though that turned out well.

I remember the snow on the road to the village squeaking at night when you walked home in the cold with your skis and ski poles on your shoulders, watching the lights and then finally seeing the buildings, and how everyone on the road said, "Grüss Gott." There were always country men in the *Weinstube* with nailed boots and mountain clothes and the air was smoky and the wooden floors were scarred by the nails. Many of the young men had served in Austrian Alpine regiments and one named Hans, who worked in the sawmill, was a famous hunter and we were good friends because we had been in the same part of the mountains in Italy. We drank together and we all sang mountain songs.

I remember the trails up through the orchards and the fields of the hillside farms above the village and the warm farm houses with their great stoves and the huge wood piles in the snow. The women worked in the kitchens carding and spinning wool into grey and black yarn. The spinning wheels worked by a foot treadle and the yarn was not dyed. The black yarn was from the wool of black sheep. The wool was natural and the fat had not been removed, and the caps and sweaters and long scarves that Hadley knitted from it never became wet in the snow.

One Christmas there was play by Hans Sachs that the school master directed. It was a good play and I wrote a review of it for the provincial paper that the hotel keeper translated. Another year a former German naval officer with a shaven head and scars came to give a lecture with lantern slides on the great and unappreciated German Victory of the Battle of Jutland. The lantern slides showed the movements of the two battle fleets and the naval officer used a billiard cue for a pointer when he pointed out the cowardice of Jellicoe and sometimes he became so angry that his voice broke. The school master was afraid that he would stab the billiard cue through the screen. Afterwards the former naval officer could not quiet himself down and everyone was ill at ease in the *Weinstube*. Only the public prosecutor and the banker drank with him, and they were at a separate table. Herr Lent, who was a Rhinelander, would not attend the lecture. There was a couple from Vienna who had come for the skiing but who did not want to go to the high mountains and so were leaving for Zurs where, I heard, they were killed in an avalanche. The man said the lecturer was the type of swine who had ruined Germany and in twenty years they would do it again. The woman with him told him to shut up in French and said this is a small place and you never know.

That was the year that so many people were killed in avalanches. The first big loss was over the mountains from our valley in Lech in the Arlberg. A party of Germans wanted to come and ski with Herr Lent on their Christmas vacations. Snow was late that year and the hills and mountain slopes were still warm from the sun when a great snowfall came. The snow was deep and powdery and it was not bound to the earth at all. Conditions for skiing could not be more dangerous and Herr Lent had wired the Berliners not to come. But it was their vacation time and they were ignorant and had no fear of avalanches. They arrived at Lech and Herr Lent refused to take them out. One man called him a coward and they said they would ski by themselves. Finally he took them to the safest slope he could find. He crossed it himself and then they followed and the whole hillside came down in a rush, rising over them as a tidal wave rises. Thirteen were dug out and nine of them were dead. The Alpine ski school had not prospered before this, and afterwards we were almost the only members. There were many people killed by avalanches that year in the Arlberg and we became great students of avalanches; the different types of avalanches, how to avoid them and how to behave if you were caught in one. Most of the writing that I did that year was in avalanche time.

The worst thing I remember of that avalanche winter was one man who was dug out. He had squatted down and made a box with his arms in front of his head, as we had been taught to do, so that there would be air to breathe as the snow rose up over you. It was a huge avalanche and it took a long time to dig everyone out, and this man was the last to be found. He had not been dead long and his neck was worn through so that the tendons and the bone were visible. He had been turning his head from side to side against the pressure of the snow. In this avalanche there must have been some old, packed snow mixed in with the new light snow that had slipped. We could not decide whether he had done it on purpose or if he had been out of his head. But there was no problem because he was refused burial in consecrated ground by the local priest anyway; since there was no proof he was a Catholic.

When we lived in Schruns I remember the long trip up the valley to the inn where we slept before setting out on the climb to the Madlener-Haus. It was a very beautiful old inn and the wood of the walls of the room where you ate and drank were silky with the years of polishing. So were the table and chairs. The food was always good and you were always hungry. You slept close together in the big bed under the feather quilt with the window open and the stars close and very bright. In the morning after breakfast you all loaded to go up the road and started the climb in the dark with the stars still bright, carrying your skis on your shoulders. The porters' skis were very short and they carried heavy loads. We competed among ourselves as to who could climb with the heaviest loads, but no one could compete with the porters, squat sullen peasants who spoke only Montafon dialect, climbed steadily like pack horses and at the top, where the Alpine Club hut was built on a shelf beside the snow-covered glacier, shed their loads against the stone wall of the hut, asked for more money than the agreed price, and, when they had obtained a compromise, shot down and away on their short skis like gnomes.

There was a wonderful German girl who skied with us. She was a great mountain skier, small and beautifully built, who could carry as heavy a rucksack as I could and carry it longer.

"Those porters always look at us as though they looked forward to bringing us down as bodies," she said. "They set the price for the climb and I've never known them not to ask for more."

The peasants of the end of the upper valley were very different from the lower and middle valley, and those of the Gauertal were as friendly as these were hostile. In the winter in Schruns I wore a beard against the sun that burned my face so badly on the high snow, and did not have a haircut, and running on skis late in the evening down the logging trails Herr Lent told me that peasants I passed on those roads above Schruns called me "the Black Christ." He said some, when they came to the *Weinstube*, called me "the

Black Kirsch-drinking Christ." But to the peasants at the far upper end of the Montafon where we hired porters to go up to the Madlener-Haus, we were all foreign devils who went into the high mountains when people should stay out of them. That we started before daylight in order not to pass avalanche places when the sun could make them dangerous was not to our credit. It only proved we were tricky as all foreign devils are.

I remember the smell of the pines and the sleeping on the mattresses of beech leaves in the woodcutters' huts and the skiing through the forest following the tracks of hares and of foxes. In the high mountains above the tree line I remember following the track of a fox until I came in sight of him and watching him stand with his forefoot raised and then go on carefully to stop and then pounce, and the whiteness and the clutter of a ptarmigan bursting out of the snow and flying away and over the ridge.

I remember all the kinds of snow that the wind could make and their different treacheries when you were on skis. Then there were the blizzards when you were in the high Alpine hut and the strange world that they would make where we had to make our route as carefully as though we had never seen the country. You had not, either, as it all was new. Finally there was the great glacier run, smooth and straight, forever straight if your legs could hold it, your ankles locked, you running so low, leaning into the speed, dropping forever and forever in the silent hiss of the crisp powder. It was better than any flying or anything else, and you built the ability to do it and to have it with the long climbs carrying the heavy rucksacks. You could not buy it nor take a ticket to the top. It was the end we worked all winter for, and all the winter built to make it possible.

The last year in the mountains new people came deep into

our lives and nothing was ever the same again. The winter of the avalanches was like a happy and innocent winter in childhood compared to that winter and the murderous summer that was to follow. Hadley and I had become too confident in each other and careless in our confidence and pride. In the mechanics of how this was penetrated I have never tried to apportion the blame, except my own part, and that was clearer all my life. The bulldozing of three people's hearts to destroy one happiness and build another and the love and the good work and all that came out of it is not part of this book. I wrote it and left it out. It is a complicated, valuable and instructive story. How it all ended, finally, has nothing to do with this either. Any blame in that was mine to take and possess and understand. The only one, Hadley, who had no possible blame, ever, came well out of it finally and married a much finer man than I ever was or could hope to be and is happy and deserves it and that was one good and lasting thing that came of that year.

Scott Fitzgerald

His talent was as natural as the pattern that was made by the dust on a butterfly's wings. At one time he understood it no more than the butterfly did and he did not know when it was brushed or marred. Later he became conscious of his damaged wings and of their construction and he learned to think. He was flying again and I was lucky to meet him just after a good time in his writing if not a good one in his life.

The first time I ever met Scott Fitzgerald a very strange thing happened. Many strange things happened with Scott but this one I was never able to forget. He had come into the Dingo bar in the rue Delambre where I was sitting with some completely worthless characters, had introduced himself and introduced a tall, pleasant man who was with him as Dunc Chaplin, the famous pitcher. I had not followed Princeton baseball and had never heard of Dunc Chaplin but he was extraordinarily nice, unworried, relaxed and friendly and I much preferred him to Scott.

Scott was a man then who looked like a boy with a face between handsome and pretty. He had very fair wavy hair, a high forehead, excited eyes and a delicate long-lipped Irish mouth that, on a girl, would have been the mouth of a beauty. His chin was well built and he had good ears and a handsome, almost beautiful, unmarked nose. This should not have added up to a pretty face, but that came from the coloring, the very fair hair and the mouth. The mouth worried you until you knew him and then it worried you more.

I was very curious to see him and I had been working very hard all day and it seemed quite wonderful that here should be Scott Fitzgerald and the great Dunc Chaplin whom I had never heard of but who was now my friend. Scott did not stop talking and since I was embarrassed by what he said—it was all about my writing and how great it was—I kept on looking at him closely and noticed instead of listening. We still went under the system, then, that praise to the face was open disgrace. Scott had ordered champagne and he and Dunc Chaplin and I drank it together with, I think, some of the worthless characters. I do not think that Dunc or I followed the speech very closely, for it was a speech; and I kept on observing Scott. He was lightly built and did not look in awfully good shape as his face was faintly puffy. His Brooks Brothers clothes fitted him well and he wore a white shirt with a buttoned-down collar and a Guard's tie. I thought I ought to tell him about the tie, maybe, because they did have British in Paris and one might come into the Dingo—there were two there at the time—but then I thought the hell with it and I looked at him some more. It turned out later he had bought the tie in Rome.

I wasn't learning very much from looking at him now except that he had well shaped, capable-looking hands, not too small, and when he sat on one of the bar stools I saw that he had very short legs. With normal legs he would have been perhaps two inches taller. We had finished the first bottle of champagne and started on the second and the speech was beginning to run down.

Both Dunc and I were beginning to feel even better than we had felt before the champagne and it was nice to have the speech over. Until then I had felt that what a great writer I was had been carefully kept secret between myself and my wife and only those people we knew well enough to speak to. I was glad Scott had come to the same happy conclusion as to this possible greatness, but I was also glad he was beginning to run out of the speech. But after the speech came the question period. You could study him and neglect to follow the speech, but the questions were un-pardoning. Scott, I was to find, believed that the novelist could find out what he needed to know by direct questioning of his friends and acquaintances. The interrogation was direct.

"Ernest," he said. "You don't mind if I call you Ernest, do you?"

"Ask Dunc," I said.

"Don't be silly. This is serious. Tell me, did you and your wife sleep together before you were married?"

"I don't know."

"What do you mean you don't know?"

"I don't remember."

"But how can you not remember something of such importance?"

"I don't know," I said. "It is odd, isn't it?"

"It's worse than odd," Scott said. "You must be able to remember."

"I'm sorry. It's a pity, isn't it?"

"Don't talk like some limey," he said. "Try to be serious and remember."

"Nope," I said. "It's hopeless."

"You could make an honest effort to remember."

The speech comes pretty high, I thought. I wondered if he gave everyone the speech, but I didn't think so because I had watched him sweat while he was making it. The sweat had come out on his long, perfect Irish upper lip in tiny drops, and that was when I had looked down away from his face and checked on the length of his legs, drawn up as he sat on the bar stool. Now I looked back at his face again and it was then that the strange thing happened.

As he sat there at the bar holding the glass of champagne the skin seemed to tighten over his face until all the puffiness was gone and then it drew tighter until the face was like a death's head. The eyes sank and began to look dead and the lips were drawn tight and the color left the face so that it was the color of used candle wax. This was not my imagination, nor have I exaggerated in describing it. His face became a true death's head, or death mask, in front of your eyes.

"Scott," I said. "Are you all right?"

He did not answer and his face looked more drawn than ever.

"We'd better get him to a first aid station," I said to Dunc Chaplin.

"No. He's all right."

"He looks like he is dying."

"No. That's the way it takes him."

We got him into a taxi and I was very worried but Dunc said he was all right and not to worry about him. "He'll probably be all right by the time he gets home," he said.

He must have been because, when I met him at the Closerie des Lilas a few days later, I said that I was sorry the stuff had hit him that way and that maybe we had drunk it too fast while we were talking.

"What do you mean you are sorry? What stuff hit me what way? What are you talking about, Ernest?"

"I meant the other night at the Dingo."

"There was nothing wrong with me at the Dingo. I simply got tired of those absolutely bloody British you were with and went home."

"There weren't any British there when you were there. Only the bartender."

"Don't try to make a mystery of it. You know the ones I mean."

"Oh," I said. He had gone back to the Dingo later. Or he'd gone there another time. No, I remembered, there had been two British there. It was true. I remembered who they were. They had been there all right.

"Yes," I said. "Of course."

"That girl with the phony title who was so rude and that silly drunk with her. They said they were friends of yours."

"They are. And she *is* very rude sometimes."

"You see. There's no use to make mysteries simply because one has drunk a few glasses of wine. Why did you want to make the mysteries? It isn't the sort of thing I thought you would do."

"I don't know." I wanted to drop it. Then I thought of something. "Were they rude about your tie?" I asked.

"Why should they have been rude about my tie? I was wearing a plain black knitted tie with a white polo shirt."

I gave up then and he asked me why I liked this café and I told him about it in the old days and he began to try to like it too and we sat there, me liking it and he trying to like it, and he asked questions and told me about writers and publishers and agents and critics and George Horace Lorimer, and the gossip and economics of being a successful writer, and he was cynical and funny and very jolly and charming and endearing, even if you were careful about anyone becoming endearing. He spoke slightingly but without bitterness of everything he had written, and I knew his new book must be very good for him to speak, without bitterness, of the faults of past books. He wanted me to read the new book, *The Great Gatsby*, as soon as he could get his last and only copy back from someone he had loaned it to. To hear him talk of it, you would never know how very good it was, except that he had the shyness about it that all non-conceited writers have when they have done something very fine, and I hoped he would get the book quickly so that I might read it.

Scott told me that he had heard from Maxwell Perkins that the book was not selling well but that it had very fine reviews. I do not remember whether it was that day, or much later, that he showed me a review by Gilbert Seldes that could not have been better. It could only have been better if Gilbert Seldes had been better. I believe it was much better later. Scott was puzzled and hurt that the book was not selling well but, as I said, he was not at all bitter then and he was both shy and happy about the book's quality.

On this day as we sat outside on the terrace of the Lilas and watched it get dusk and the people passing on the sidewalk and the thin grey light of the evening changing, there was no chemical change in him from the two whisky and sodas that we drank. I watched carefully for it, but it did not come and he asked no shameless questions, did nothing embarrassing, made no speeches, and acted as a normal, intelligent and charming person.

He told me that he and Zelda, his wife, had been compelled to abandon their small Renault motor car in Lyon because of bad weather and he asked me if I would go down to Lyon with him on the train to pick up the car and drive up with him to Paris. The Fitzgeralds had rented a furnished flat at 14 rue de Tilsitt not far from the Etoile. It was late spring now and I thought the country would be at its best and we could have an excellent trip. Scott seemed so nice and so reasonable, and I had watched him drink two good solid whiskies and nothing happened, and his charm and his seeming good sense made the other night at the Dingo seem like an unpleasant dream. So I said I would like to go down to Lyon with him and when did he want to leave.

We agreed to meet the next day and we then arranged to leave for Lyon on the express train that left in the morning. This train left at a convenient hour and was very fast. It made only one stop, I believe, at Dijon. We planned to get into Lyon, have the car checked and in good shape, have an excellent dinner and get an early-morning start back towards Paris. We set a tentative date for leaving and I saw him again twice, we made a final date, and checked it the night before.

I was enthusiastic about the trip and my wife thought it was a splendid idea. I would have the company of an older and successful writer, and in the time we would have to talk in the car I would certainly learn much that it would be useful to know. It is strange now to remember thinking of Scott as an older writer, but at the time, since I had not yet read *The Great Gatsby,* I thought of him as a much older writer who had written a very silly, badly written and collegiate book followed by another book I had been unable to read. I thought he wrote *Saturday Evening Post* stories that had been readable three years before but I never thought of him as a serious writer. He had told me at the Closerie des Lilas how he wrote what he thought were good stories, and which really were good stories for the *Post,* and then changed them for submission, knowing exactly how he must make the twists that made them into salable magazine stories. I had been shocked at this and I said I thought it was whoreing. He said it was whoreing but that he had to do it as he made his money from the magazines to have money ahead to write decent books. I said that I did not believe anyone could write any way except the very best they could write without destroying their talent. He said he had learned to write the stories for the *Post* so that they did him no harm at all. He wrote the real story first, he said, and the destruction and changing did him no harm. I could not believe this and I wanted to argue him out of it but I needed a novel to back up my faith and to show him and convince him, and I had not yet written any such novel. Since I had started to break all my writing down and get rid of all facility and try to make instead of describe, writing had been wonderful to do. But it was very difficult, and I did not know how I would ever write anything as long as a novel. It often took me a full morning of work to write a paragraph.

My wife, Hadley, was happy for me to make the trip, though she did not take seriously the writing of Scott's that she had read. Her idea of a good writer was Henry James. But she thought it was a good idea for me to take a rest from work and make the trip, although we both wished that we had enough money to have a car and were making the trip ourselves. But that was something I never had any idea would happen. I had received an advance of two hundred dollars from Boni and Liveright for a first book of short stories to be published in America that fall, and I was selling stories to the *Frankfurter Zeitung* and to *Der Querschnitt* in Berlin and to *This Quarter* and *The Transatlantic Review* in Paris and we were living with great economy and not spending any money except for necessities in order to save money to go down to the *feria* at Pamplona in July and to Madrid and to the *feria* in Valencia afterwards.

On the morning we were to leave from the Gare de Lyon I arrived in plenty of time and waited outside the train gates for Scott. He was bringing the tickets. When it got close to the time for the train to leave and he had not arrived, I bought an entry ticket to the track and walked along the side of the train looking for him. I did not see him and as the long train was about to pull out I got aboard and walked through the train hoping only, by now, that he would be aboard. It was a long train and he was not on it. I explained the situation to the conductor, paid for a ticket, second class—there was no third—and asked the conductor for the name of the best hotel in Lyon. There was nothing to do but wire Scott from Dijon giving him the address of the hotel where I would wait for him in Lyon. He would not get it before he left, but his wife would be presumed to wire it on to him. I had never heard, then, of a grown man missing a train; but on this trip I was to learn many new things.

In those days I had a very bad, quick temper, but by the time we were through Montereau it had quieted down and I was not too angry to watch and enjoy the countryside and at noon I had a good lunch in the dining car and drank a bottle of St.-Émilion and thought that even if I had been a damned fool to accept an invitation for a trip that was to be paid for by someone else, and was spending money on it that we needed to go to Spain, it was a good lesson for me. I had never before accepted an invitation to go on any trip that was paid for, instead of the cost split, and in this one I had insisted that we split the cost of the hotels and meals. But now I did not know whether Fitzgerald would even show up. While I had been angry I had demoted him from Scott to Fitzgerald. Later I was delighted that I had used up the anger at the start and gotten it over with. It was not a trip designed for a man easy to anger.

In Lyon I learned that Scott had left Paris for Lyon but had left no word as to where he was staying. I confirmed my address there and the servant said she would let him know if he called. Madame was not well and was still sleeping. I called all the name hotels and left messages but could not locate Scott and then I went out to a café to have an aperitif and read the papers. At the café I met a man who ate fire for a living and also bent coins which he held in his toothless jaws with his thumb and forefinger. His gums were sore but firm to the eye as he exhibited them and he said it was not a bad *métier*. I asked him to have a drink and he was pleased. He had a fine dark face that glowed and shone when he ate the fire. He said there was no money in eating fire nor in feats of strength with fingers and jaws in Lyon. False fire-eaters had ruined the *métier* and would continue to ruin it wherever they were allowed to practice. He had been eating fire all evening, he said, and did not have enough money on him to eat anything else that night. I asked him to have another drink, to wash away the petrol taste of the fire-eating, and said we could have dinner together if he knew a good place that was cheap enough. He said he knew an excellent place.

We ate very cheaply in an Algerian restaurant and I liked the food and the Algerian wine. The fire-eater was a nice man and it was interesting to see him eat, as he could chew with his gums as well as most people can with their teeth. He asked me what I did to make a living and I told him that I was starting in as a writer. He asked what sort of writing and I told him stories. He said he knew many stories, some of them more horrible and incredible than anything that had ever been written. He could tell them to me and I would write them and then if they made any money I would give him whatever I thought fair. Better still we could go to North Africa together and he would take me to the country of the Blue Sultan where I could get stories such as no man had ever heard.

I asked him what sort of stories and he said battles, executions, tortures, violations, fearful customs, unbelievable practices, debaucheries; anything I needed. It was getting time for me to get back to the hotel and check on Scott again, so I paid for the meal and said we would certainly be running into each other again. He said he was working down toward Marseilles and I said sooner or later we would meet somewhere and it was a pleasure to have dined together. I left him straightening out bent coins and stacking them on the table and walked back to the hotel.

Lyon was not a very cheerful town at night. It was a big, heavy, solid-money town, probably fine if you had money and liked that sort of town. For years I had heard about the wonderful chicken in the restaurants there, but we had eaten mutton instead. The mutton had been excellent.

There was no word from Scott at the hotel and I went to bed in the unaccustomed luxury of the hotel and read a copy of the first volume of *A Sportsman's Sketches* by Turgenev that I had borrowed from Sylvia Beach's library. I had not been in the heavy luxury of a big hotel for three years and I opened the windows wide and rolled up the pillows under my back and head and was happy being with Turgenev in Russia until I was asleep while still reading. I was shaving in the morning getting ready to go out for breakfast when they called from the desk saying a gentleman was downstairs to see me.

"Ask him to come up, please," I said and went on shaving, listening to the town which had come heavily alive since early morning.

Scott did not come up and I met him down at the desk.

"I'm terribly sorry there was this mix-up," he said. "If I had only known what hotel you were going to it would have been simple."

"That's all right," I said. We were going to have a long ride and I was all for peace. "What train did you come down on?"

"One not long after the one you took. It was a very comfortable train and we might just as well have come down together."

"Have you had breakfast?"

"Not yet. I've been hunting all over the town for you."

"That's a shame," I said. "Didn't they tell you at home that I was here?"

"No. Zelda wasn't feeling well and I probably shouldn't have come. The whole trip has been disastrous so far."

"Let's get some breakfast and find the car and roll," I said.

"That's fine. Should we have breakfast here?"

"It would be quicker in a café."

"But we're sure to get a good breakfast here."

"All right."

It was a big American breakfast with ham and eggs and it was very good. But by the time we had ordered it, waited for it, eaten it, and waited to pay for it, close to an hour had been lost. It was not until the waiter came with the bill that Scott decided that we have the hotel make us a picnic lunch. I tried to argue him out of this as I was sure we could get a bottle of Mâcon in Mâcon and we could buy something to make sandwiches in a *charcuterie*. Or, if things were closed when we went through, there would be any number of restaurants where we could stop on our way. But he said I had told him that the chicken was wonderful in Lyon and that we should certainly take one with us. So the hotel made us a lunch that could not have cost us very much more than four or five times what it would have cost us if we had bought it ourselves.

Scott had obviously been drinking before I met him and, as he looked as though he needed a drink, I asked him if he did not want one in the bar before we set out. He told me he was not a morning drinker and asked if I was. I told him it depended entirely on how I felt and what I had to do and he said that if I felt that I needed a drink, he would keep me company so I would not have to drink alone. So we had a whisky and Perrier in the bar while we waited for the lunch and both felt much better.

I paid for the hotel room and the bar, although Scott wanted to pay for everything. Since the start of the trip I had felt a little complicated about it emotionally and I found I felt much better the more things I could pay for. I was using up money we had saved for Spain, but I knew I had good credit with Sylvia Beach and could borrow and repay whatever I was wasting now.

At the garage where Scott had left the car, it was astonishing to find that the small Renault had no top. The top had been damaged in unloading the car in Marseilles, or it had been damaged in Marseilles in some manner—Scott explained it a little vaguely—and Zelda had ordered it cut away and refused to have it replaced. His wife hated car tops, Scott told me, and without the top they had driven as far as Lyon where they were halted by the rain. The car was in fair shape otherwise and Scott paid the bill after disputing several charges for washing, greasing, and for adding two liters of oil. The garage man explained to me that the car needed new piston rings and had evidently been run without sufficient oil and water. He showed me how it had heated up and burned the paint off the motor. He said if I could persuade Monsieur to have a ring job done in Paris, the car, which was a good little car, would be able to give the service it was built for if it was cared for at all.

"Monsieur would not let me replace the top."

"No?"

"One has an obligation to a vehicle."

"One has."

"You gentlemen have no waterproofs?"

"No," I said. "I did not know about the top."

"Try and make Monsieur be serious," he said pleadingly. "At least about the vehicle."

"Ah," I said.

We were halted by rain about an hour north of Lyon.

In that day we were halted by rain possibly ten times. They were passing showers and some of them were longer than others. If we had waterproof coats it would have been pleasant enough to drive in that spring rain. As it was we sought the shelter of trees or halted at cafés alongside the road. We had a marvelous lunch from the hotel at Lyon, an excellent truffled roast chicken, delicious bread and white Mâcon wine and Scott was very happy when we drank the white Mâconnais at each of our stops. At Mâcon I had bought four more bottles of excellent wine which I uncorked as we needed them.

I am not sure Scott had ever drunk wine from a bottle before and it was exciting to him as though he were slumming or as a girl might be excited by going swimming for the first time without a bathing suit. But, by early afternoon, he had begun to worry about his health. He told me about two people who had died of congestion of the lungs recently. Both of them had died in Italy and he had been deeply impressed.

I told him that congestion of the lungs was an old-fashioned term for pneumonia, and he told me that I knew nothing about it and was absolutely wrong. Congestion of the lungs was a malady which was indigenous to Europe and I could not possibly know anything about it even if I had read my father's medical books, since they dealt with diseases that were strictly American. I said that my father had studied in Europe too. But Scott explained that congestion of the lungs had only appeared in Europe recently and that my father could not possibly have known anything about it. He also explained that diseases were different in different parts of America, and if my father had practiced medicine in New York instead of in the Middle West, he would have known an entirely different gamut of diseases. He used the word gamut.

I said that he had a good point in the prevalence of certain diseases in one part of the United States and their absence in others and cited the amount of leprosy in New Orleans and its low incidence, then, in Chicago. But I said that doctors had a system of exchange of knowledge and information among themselves and now that I remembered it after he had brought it up, I had read the authoritative article on congestion of the lungs in Europe in the *Journal of the American Medical Association* which traced its history back to Hippocrates himself. This held him for a while and I urged him to take another drink of Mâcon, since a good white wine, moderately full-bodied but with a low alcoholic content, was almost a specific against the disease.

Scott cheered a little after this but he began to fail again shortly and asked me if we would make a big town before the onset of the fever and delirium by which, I had told him, the true congestion of the lungs, European, announced itself. I was now translating from an article which I had read in a French medical journal on the same malady while waiting at the American Hospital in Neuilly to have my throat cauterized, I told him. A word like cauterized had a comforting effect on Scott. But he wanted to know when we would make the town. I said if we pushed on we should make it in twenty-five minutes to an hour.

Scott then asked me if I were afraid to die and I said more at some times than at others.

It now began to rain really heavily and we took refuge in

the next village at a café. I cannot remember all the details of that afternoon but when we were finally in a hotel at what must have been Châlon-sur-Saône, it was so late that the drug stores were closed. Scott had undressed and gone to bed as soon as we reached the hotel. He did not mind dying of congestion of the lungs, he said. It was only the question of who was to look after Zelda and young Scotty. I did not see very well how I could look after them since I was having a healthily rough time looking after my wife Hadley and young son Bumby, but I said I would do my best and Scott thanked me. I must see that Zelda did not drink and that Scotty should have an English governess.

We had sent our clothes to be dried and were in our pajamas. It was still raining outside but it was cheerful in the room with the electric light on. Scott was lying in bed to conserve his strength for his battle against the disease. I had taken his pulse, which was seventy-two, and had felt his forehead, which was cool. I had listened to his chest and had him breathe deeply, and his chest sounded all right.

"Look, Scott," I said. "You're perfectly O.K. If you want to do the best thing to keep from catching cold, just stay in bed and I'll order us each a lemonade and a whisky and you take an aspirin with yours and you'll feel fine and won't even get a cold in your head."

"Those old wives' remedies," Scott said.

"You haven't any temperature. How the hell are you going to have congestion of the lungs without a temperature?"

"Don't swear at me," Scott said. "How do you know I haven't a temperature?"

"Your pulse is normal and you haven't any fever to the touch."

"To the touch," Scott said bitterly. "If you're a real friend, get me a thermometer."

"I'm in pajamas."

"Send for one."

I rang for the waiter. He didn't come and I rang again and then went down the hallway to look for him. Scott was lying with his eyes closed, breathing slowly and carefully and, with his waxy color and his perfect features, he looked like a little dead crusader. I was getting tired of the literary life, if this was the literary life that I was leading, and already I missed not working and I felt the death loneliness that comes at the end of every day that is wasted in your life. I was very tired of Scott and of this silly comedy, but I found the waiter and gave him money to buy a thermometer and a tube of aspirin, and ordered two *citron pressés* and two double whiskies. I tried to order a bottle of whisky but they would only sell it by the drink.

Back in the room Scott was still lying as though on his tomb, sculpted as a monument to himself, his eyes closed and breathing with exemplary dignity.

Hearing me come in the room, he spoke. "Did you get the thermometer?"

I went over and put my hand on his forehead. It was not as cold as the tomb. But it was cool and not clammy.

"Nope," I said.

"I thought you'd brought it."

"I sent out for it."

"It's not the same thing."

"No. It isn't, is it?"

You could not be angry with Scott any more than you could be angry with someone who was crazy, but I was getting angry with myself for having become involved in the whole silliness. He did have a point though, and I knew it very well. Most drunkards in those days died of pneumonia, a disease which has now been almost eliminated. But it was hard to accept him as a drunkard, since he was affected by such small quantities of alcohol.

In Europe then we thought of wine as something as healthy and normal as food and also as a great giver of happiness and well-being and delight. Drinking wine was not a snobbism nor a sign of sophistication nor a cult; it was as natural as eating and to me as necessary, and I would not have thought of eating a meal without drinking either wine or cider or beer. I loved all wines except sweet or sweetish wines and wines that were too heavy, and it had never occurred to me that sharing a few bottles of fairly light, dry, white Mâcon could cause chemical changes in Scott that would turn him into a fool. There had been the whisky and Perrier in the morning but, in my ignorance of alcoholics then, I could not imagine that harming anyone who was driving in an open car in the rain. The alcohol should have been oxidized in a very short time.

While waiting for the waiter to bring the various things I sat and read a paper and finished one of the bottles of Mâcon that had been uncorked at the last stop. When you live in France there are always some splendid crimes in the newspapers that you follow from day to day. These crimes read like continued stories and it is necessary to have read the opening chapters, since there are no summaries provided as there are in American serial stories and, anyway, no serial is as good in an American periodical unless you have read the all-important first chapter. When you are traveling through France the papers are disappointing because you miss the continuity of the different *crimes, affaires,* or *scandales,* and you miss much of the pleasure to be derived from reading about them in a café. Tonight I would have much preferred to be in a café where I might read the morning editions of the Paris papers and watch the people and drink something a little more authoritative than the Mâcon in preparation for dinner. But I was riding herd on Scott so I enjoyed myself where I was.

When the waiter arrived with the two glasses with the pressed lemon juice and ice, the whiskies, and the bottle of Perrier water, he told me that the pharmacy was closed and he could not get a thermometer. He had borrowed some aspirin. I asked him to see if he could borrow a thermometer. Scott opened his eyes and gave a baleful Irish look at the waiter.

"Have you told him how serious it is?" he asked.

"I think he understands."

"Please try to make it clear."

I tried to make it clear and the waiter said, "I'll bring what I can."

"Did you tip him enough to do any good? They only work for tips."

"I didn't know that," I said. "I thought the hotel paid them something on the side."

"I mean they will only do something for you for a substantial tip. Most of them are rotten clean through."

I thought of Evan Shipman and I thought of the waiter at the Closerie des Lilas who had been forced to cut his mustache when they made the American bar at the Closerie, and how Evan had been working out at his garden in Montrouge long before I had met Scott, and what good friends we all were and had been for a long time at the Lilas and of all of the moves that had been made and what they meant to all of us. I thought of telling Scott about this whole problem of the Lilas, although I had probably mentioned it to him before, but I knew he did not care about waiters nor their problems nor their great kindnesses and affections. At that time Scott hated the French, and since almost the only French he met with regularly were waiters whom he did not understand, taxi-drivers, garage employees and landlords, he had many opportunities to insult and abuse them.

He hated the Italians even more than the French and could not talk about them calmly even when he was sober. The English he often hated but he sometimes tolerated them and occasionally looked up to them. I do not know how he felt about the Germans and the Austrians. I do not know whether he had ever met any then or any Swiss.

On this evening in the hotel I was delighted that he was being so calm. I had mixed the lemonade and whisky and given it to him with two aspirins and he had swallowed the aspirins without protest and with admirable calm and was sipping his drink. His eyes were open now and were looking far away. I was reading the *crime* in the inside of the paper and was quite happy, too happy it seemed.

"You're a cold one, aren't you?" Scott asked and looking at him I saw that I had been wrong in my prescription, if not in my diagnosis, and that the whisky was working against us.

"How do you mean, Scott?"

"You can sit there and read that dirty French rag of a paper and it doesn't mean a thing to you that I am dying."

"Do you want me to call a doctor?"

"No. I don't want a dirty French provincial doctor."

"What do you want?"

"I want my temperature taken. Then I want my clothes dried and for us to get on an express train for Paris and to go to the American hospital at Neuilly."

"Our clothes won't be dry until morning and there aren't any express trains," I said. "Why don't you rest and have some dinner in bed?"

"I want my temperature taken."

After this went on for a long time the waiter brought a thermometer.

"Is this the only one you could get?" I asked. Scott had shut his eyes when the waiter came in and he did look at least as far gone as Camille. I have never seen a man who lost the blood from his face so fast and I wondered where it went.

"It is the only one in the hotel," the waiter said and handed me the thermometer. It was a bath thermometer with a wooden back and enough metal to sink it in the bath. I took a quick gulp of the whisky sour and opened the window a moment to look out at the rain. When I turned Scott was watching me.

I shook the thermometer down professionally and said, "You're lucky it's not a rectal thermometer."

"Where does this kind go?"

"Under the arm," I told him and tucked it under my arm.

"Don't upset the temperature," Scott said. I shook the thermometer again with a single sharp downward twitch and unbuttoned his pajama jacket and put the instrument under his armpit while I felt his cool forehead and then took his pulse. He stared straight ahead. The pulse was seventy-two. I kept the thermometer in for four minutes.

"I thought they only kept them in for one minute," Scott said.

"This is a big thermometer," I explained. "You multiply by the square of the size of the thermometer. It's a centigrade thermometer."

Finally I took the thermometer out and carried it over by the reading light.

"What is it?"

"Thirty-seven and six-tenths."

"What's normal?"

"That's normal."

"Are you sure?"

"Sure."

"Try it on yourself. I have to be sure."

I shook the thermometer down and opened my pajamas and put the thermometer in my armpit and held it there while I watched the time. Then I looked at it.

"What is it?" I studied it.

"Exactly the same."

"How do you feel?"

"Splendid," I said. I was trying to remember whether thirty-seven six was really normal or not. It did not matter, for the thermometer, unaffected, was steady at thirty.

Scott was a little suspicious so I asked if he wanted me to make another test.

"No," he said. "We can be happy it cleared up so quickly. I've always had great recuperative power."

"You're fine," I said. "But I think it would be just as well if you stayed in bed and had a light supper, and then we can start early in the morning." I had planned to buy us raincoats but I would have to borrow money from him for that and I did not want to start arguing about that now.

Scott did not want to stay in bed. He wanted to get up and get dressed and go downstairs and call Zelda so she would know he was all right.

"Why would she think you weren't all right?"

"This is the first night I have ever slept away from her since we were married and I have to talk to her. You can see what it means to us both, can't you?"

I could, but I could not see how he and Zelda could have slept together on the night just past; but it was nothing to argue about. Scott drank the whisky sour down very fast now and asked me to order another. I found the waiter and returned the thermometer and asked him how our clothes were coming along. He thought they might be dry in an hour

1. Ernest Hemingway as a young man

2. Hadley and Ernest Hemingway

3. Gertrude Stein in her Paris apartment,
   27 rue de Fleurus

4. Sylvia Beach and Ernest Hemingway in front of her
bookshop, Shakespeare and Company

OPPOSITE

5. TOP: Interior of the bookshop showing
James Joyce, with Sylvia Beach and
Adrienne Monnier

6. BOTTOM: In Ezra Pound's studio: Ezra
Pound, Ford Madox Ford, James Joyce;
standing John Quinn

7. Ernest Hemingway and Bumby

8. Zelda, Scott Fitzgerald and Scotty

9. Ernest Hemingway in the late 1920s

or so. "Have the valet press them and that will dry them. It doesn't matter that they should be bone-dry."

The waiter brought the two drinks against catching cold and I sipped mine and urged Scott to sip his slowly. I was worried now he might catch cold and I could see by now that if he ever had anything as definitely bad as a cold he would probably have to be hospitalized. But the drink made him feel wonderful for a while and he was happy with the tragic implications of this being Zelda's and his first night of separation since their marriage. Finally he could not wait longer to call her and put on his dressing gown and went down to put the call through.

It would take some time for the call and shortly after he came up, the waiter appeared with two more double whisky sours. This was the most I had ever seen Scott drink until then, but they had no effect on him except to make him more animated and talkative, and he started to tell me the outline of his life with Zelda. He told me how he had first met her during the war and then lost her and won her back, and about their marriage and then about something tragic that had happened to them at St.-Raphael about a year ago. This first version that he told me of Zelda and a French naval aviator falling in love was a truly sad story and I believe it was a true story. Later he told me other versions of it as though trying them for use in a novel, but none was as sad as this first one and I always believed the first one, although any of them might have been true. They were better told each time; but they never hurt you the same way the first one did.

Scott was very articulate and told a story well. He did not have to spell the words nor attempt to punctuate and you did not have the feeling of reading an illiterate that his letters gave you before they had been corrected. I knew him for two years before he could spell my name; but then it was a long name to spell and perhaps it became harder to spell all of the time, and I give him great credit for spelling it correctly finally. He learned to spell many more important things and he tried to think straight about many more.

On this night though he wanted me to know and understand and appreciate what it was that had happened at St.-Raphael and I saw it so clearly that I could see the single seater seaplane buzzing the diving raft and the color of the sea and the shape of the pontoons and the shadow that they cast and Zelda's tan and Scott's tan and the dark blonde and the light blonde of their hair and the darkly tanned face of the boy that was in love with Zelda. I could not ask the question that was in my mind, how, if this story was true and it had all happened, could Scott have slept each night in the same bed with Zelda? But maybe that was what had made it sadder than any story anyone had ever told me then, and, too, maybe he did not remember, as he did not remember last night.

Our clothes came before the call did and we dressed and went downstairs to have dinner. Scott was a little unsteady now and he looked at people out of the side of his eyes with a certain belligerency. We had very good snails, with a carafe of Fleurie to start with and while we were about halfway through them Scott's call came. He was gone about an hour and I ate his snails finally, dipping up the butter, garlic and parsley sauce with broken bits of bread, and drank the carafe of Fleurie. When he came back I said I would get him some more snails but he said he did not want any. He wanted something simple. He did not want a steak, nor liver and bacon, nor an omelette. He would take chicken. We had eaten very good cold chicken at noon but this was still famous chicken country, so we had *poularde de Bresse* and a bottle of Montagny, a light, pleasant white wine of the neighborhood. Scott ate very little and sipped at one glass of the wine. He passed out at the table with his head on his hands. It was natural and there was no theater about it and it even looked as though he were careful not to spill nor break things. The waiter and I got him up to his room and laid him on the bed and I undressed him to his underwear, hung his clothes up, and then stripped the covers off the bed and spread them over him. I opened the window and saw it was clear outside and left the window open.

Downstairs I finished my dinner and thought about Scott. It was obvious he should not drink anything and I had not been taking good care of him. Anything that he drank seemed to stimulate him too much and then to poison him and I planned on the next day to cut all drinking to the minimum. I would tell him that we were getting back to Paris now and that I had to train in order to write. This was not true. My training was never to drink after dinner nor before I wrote nor while I was writing. But I went upstairs and opened all the windows wide and undressed and was asleep almost as soon as I was in bed.

The next day we drove to Paris on a beautiful day up through the Côte d'Or with the air freshly washed and the hills and the fields and the vineyards all new, and Scott was very cheerful and happy and healthy and told me the plots of each and every one of Michael Arlen's books. Michael Arlen, he said, was the man you had to watch and he and I could both learn much from him. I said I could not read the books. He said I did not have to. He would tell me the plots and describe the characters. He gave me a sort of oral Ph.D. thesis on Michael Arlen.

I asked him if he had a good connection on the phone when he talked to Zelda and he said that it was not bad and that they had many things to talk about. At meals I ordered one bottle of the lightest wine I could locate and told Scott he would do me a great favor if he would not let me order any more as I had to train before I wrote and should not under any circumstances drink more than half a bottle. He co-operated wonderfully and when he saw me looking nervous toward the end of a single bottle, gave me some of his share.

When I had left him at his home and taken a taxi back to the sawmill, it was wonderful to see my wife and we went up to the Closerie des Lilas to have a drink. We were happy the way children are who have been separated and are together again and I told her about the trip.

"But didn't you have any fun or learn anything, Tatie?" she asked.

"I learned about Michael Arlen, if I would have listened, and I learned things I haven't sorted out."

"Isn't Scott happy at all?"

"Maybe."

"Poor man."

"I learned one thing."

"What?"

"Never to go on trips with anyone you do not love."

"Isn't that fine?"

"Yes. And we're going to Spain."

"Yes. Now it's less than six weeks before we go. And this year we won't let anyone spoil it, will we?"

"No. And after Pamplona we'll go to Madrid and to Valencia."

"M-m-m-m," she said softly, like a cat.

"Poor Scott," I said.

"Poor everybody," Hadley said. "Rich feathercats with no money."

"We're awfully lucky."

"We'll have to be good and hold it."

We both touched wood on the café table and the waiter came to see what it was we wanted. But what we wanted not he, nor anyone else, nor knocking on wood nor on marble, as this café table-top was, could ever bring us. But we did not know it that night and we were very happy.

A day or two after the trip Scott brought his book over. It had a garish dust jacket and I remember being embarrassed by the violence, bad taste and slippery look of it. It looked the book jacket for a book of bad science fiction. Scott told me not to be put off by it, that it had to do with a billboard along a highway in Long Island that was important in the story. He said he had liked the jacket and now he didn't like it. I took it off to read the book.

When I had finished the book I knew that no matter what Scott did, nor how preposterously he behaved, I must know it was like a sickness and be of any help I could to him and try to be a good friend. He had many good, good friends, more than anyone I knew. But I enlisted as one more, whether I could be of any use to him or not. If he could write a book as fine as *The Great Gatsby* I was sure that he could write an even better one. I did not know Zelda yet, and so I did not know the terrible odds that were against him. But we were to find them out soon enough.

18

Hawks Do Not Share

Scott Fitzgerald invited us to have lunch with his wife Zelda and his little daughter at the furnished flat they had rented at 14 rue de Tilsitt. I cannot remember much about the flat except that it was gloomy and airless and that there was nothing in it that seemed to belong to them except Scott's first books bound in light blue leather with the titles in gold. Scott also showed us a large ledger with all of the stories he had published listed in it year after year with the prices he had received for them and also the amounts received for any motion picture sales, and the sales and royalties of his books. They were all noted as carefully as the log of a ship and Scott showed them to both of us with impersonal pride as though he were the curator of a museum. Scott was nervous and hospitable and he showed us his accounts of his earnings as though they had been the view. There was no view.

Zelda had a very bad hangover. They had been up on Montmartre the night before and had quarreled because Scott did not want to get drunk. He had decided, he told me, to work hard and not to drink and Zelda was treating him as though he were a kill-joy or a spoilsport. Those were the two words she used to him and there was recrimination and Zelda would say, "I did not. I did no such thing. It's not true, Scott." Later she would seem to recall something and would laugh happily.

On this day Zelda did not look her best. Her beautiful

dark blonde hair had been ruined temporarily by a bad permanent she had gotten in Lyon, where the rain had made them abandon their car, and her eyes were tired and her face was too taut and drawn.

She was formally pleasant to Hadley and me but a big part of her seemed not to be present but to still be on the party she had come home from that morning. She and Scott both seemed to feel that Scott and I had enjoyed a great and wonderful time on the trip up from Lyon and she was jealous about it.

"When you two can go off and have such simply wonderful times together, it only seems fair that I should have just a little fun with our good friends here in Paris," she said to Scott.

Scott was being the perfect host and we ate a very bad lunch that the wine cheered a little but not much. The little girl was blonde, chubby-faced, well built, and very healthy looking and spoke English with a strong Cockney accent. Scott explained that she had an English nanny because he wanted her to speak like Lady Diana Manners when she grew up.

Zelda had hawk's eyes and a thin mouth and deep-south manners and accent. Watching her face you could see her mind leave the table and go to the night's party and return with her eyes blank as a cat's and then pleased, and the pleasure would show along the thin line of her lips and then be gone. Scott was being the good cheerful host and Zelda looked at him and she smiled happily with her eyes and her mouth too as he drank the wine. I learned to know that smile very well. It meant she knew Scott would not be able to write.

Zelda was very jealous of Scott's work and as we got to know them, this fell into a regular pattern. Scott would resolve not to go on all-night drinking parties and to get some exercise each day and work regularly. He would start to work and as soon as he was working well Zelda would begin complaining about how bored she was and get him off on another drunken party. They would quarrel and then make up and he would sweat out the alcohol on long walks with me, and make up his mind that this time he would really work, and would start off well. Then it would start all over again.

Scott was very much in love with Zelda and he was very jealous of her. He told me many times on our walks of how she had fallen in love with a French navy pilot. He had told me the story very many times by now starting on the trip and it was his best story no matter how he told it. But she had never made him really jealous with another man since. This spring she was making him jealous with other women and on the Montmartre parties he was afraid to pass out and he was afraid to have her pass out. Becoming unconscious when they drank had always been their great defense. They went to sleep on drinking an amount of liquor or champagne that would have little effect on a person accustomed to drinking, and they would go to sleep like children. I have seen them become unconscious not as though they were drunk but as though they had been anesthetized and their friends, or sometimes a taxi-driver, would get them to bed, and when they woke they would be fresh and happy, not having taken enough alcohol to damage their bodies before it made them unconscious.

Now they had lost this natural defense. At this time Zelda could drink more than Scott could and Scott was afraid for her to pass out in the company they kept that spring and in the places they went to. Scott did not like the places nor the people and he had to drink more than he could drink and be in any control of himself, to stand the people and the places, and then he began to have to drink to keep awake after he would usually have passed out. Finally he had few intervals of work at all.

He was always trying to work. Each day he would try and fail. He laid the failure to Paris, the town best organized for a writer to write in that there is, and he thought always that there would be some place where he and Zelda could have a good life together again. He thought of the Riviera, as it was then before it had all been built up, with the lovely stretches of blue sea and the sand beaches and the stretches of pine woods and the mountains of the Esterel going out into the sea. He remembered it as it was when he and Zelda had first found it before people went there for the summer.

Scott told me about the Riviera and how my wife and I must come there the next summer and how we would go there and how he would find a place for us that was not expensive and we would both work hard every day and swim and lie on the beach and be brown and only have a single apéritif before lunch and one before dinner. Zelda would be happy there, he said. She loved to swim and was a beautiful diver and she was happy with that life and would want him to work and everything would be wonderful. He and Zelda and their daughter were going to go there that summer.

I was trying to get him to write his stories as well as he could and not trick them to conform to any formula, as he had explained that he did.

"You've written a fine novel now," I told him. "And you mustn't write slop."

"The novel isn't selling," he said. "I must write stories and they have to be stories that will sell."

"Write the best story that you can and write it as straight as you can."

"I'm going to," he said.

But the way things were going, he was lucky to get any work done at all. Zelda did not encourage the people who were chasing her and she had nothing to do with them, she said. But it amused her and it made Scott jealous and he had to go with her to the places. It destroyed his work, and she was more jealous of his work than anything.

All that late spring and early summer Scott fought to work but he could only work in snatches. When I saw him he was always cheerful, sometimes desperately cheerful, and he made good jokes and was a good companion. When he had very bad times, I listened to him about them and tried to make him know that if he could hold onto himself he would write as he was made to write, and that only death was irrevocable. He would make fun of himself then, and as long as he could do that I thought that he was safe. Through all of this he wrote one good story, "The Rich Boy," and I was sure that he could write better than that as he did later.

During the summer we were in Spain and I started the first draft of a novel and finished it back in Paris in September. Scott and Zelda had been at Cap d'Antibes, and that fall when I saw him in Paris he was very changed. He had not done any sobering up on the Riviera and he was drunk now in the day time as well as nights. It did not make any difference any more to him that anyone was working and he would come to 113 rue Notre-Dame-des-Champs any time he was drunk either in the day time or at night. He had begun to be very rude to his inferiors or anyone he considered his inferior.

One time he came in through the sawmill gate with his

small daughter—it was the English nurse's day off and Scott was caring for the child—and at the foot of the stairs she told him she needed to go to bathroom. Scott started to undress her and the proprietor, who lived on the floor below us, came in and said very politely, "Monsieur, there is a *cabinet de toilette* just ahead of you to the left of the stairs."

"Yes, and I'll put your head in it too, if you're not too careful," Scott told him.

He was very difficult all that fall but he had begun to work on a novel when he was sober. I saw him rarely when he was sober, but when he was sober he was always pleasant and he still made jokes and sometimes he would still make jokes about himself. But when he was drunk he would usually come to find me and, drunk, he took almost as much pleasure interfering with my work as Zelda did interfering with his. This continued for years but, for years too, I had no more loyal friend than Scott when he was sober.

That fall of 1925 he was upset because I would not show him the manuscript of the first draft of *The Sun Also Rises*. I explained to him that it would mean nothing until I had gone over it and rewritten it and that I did not want to discuss it or show it to anyone first. We were going down to Schruns in the Vorarlberg in Austria as soon as the first snowfall there.

I rewrote the first half of the manuscript there, finishing it in January, I think. I took it to New York and showed it to Max Perkins of Scribner's and then went back to Schruns and finished rewriting the book. Scott did not see it until after the completed rewritten and cut manuscript had been sent to Scribner's at the end of April. I do not remember when I showed finished things to him first that year nor when he first saw the proofs on the rewritten and cut version. We discussed them. But I made the decisions. Not that it matters. I remembered joking with him about them and him being worried and anxious to help as always once a thing was done. But I did not want his help while I was trying to do it.

While we were living in the Vorarlberg and I was finishing rewriting the novel, Scott and his wife and child had left Paris for a watering place in the lower Pyrénées. Zelda had been ill with that familiar intestinal complaint that too much champagne produces and which was then diagnosed as colitis. Scott was not drinking, and starting to work and he wanted us, really, to come to Juan-les-Pins in June. They would find an inexpensive villa for us and this time he would not drink and it would be like the old good days and we would swim and be healthy and brown and have one apéritif before lunch and one before dinner. Zelda was well again and they were both fine and his novel was going wonderfully. He had money coming in from a dramatization of *The Great Gatsby* which was running well and it would sell to the movies and he had no worries. Zelda was really fine and everything was going to be wonderful.

I had been down in Madrid in May working by myself and I came by train from Bayonne to Juan-les-Pins third class and quite hungry because I had run out of money stupidly and had eaten last in Hendaye at the French-Spanish frontier. It was a nice villa and Scott had a very fine house not far away and I was very happy to see my wife who had the villa running beautifully, and our friends, and the single aperitif before lunch was very good and we had several more. That night there was a party to welcome us at the Casino, just a small party, the MacLeishes, the Murphys, the Fitzgeralds and we who were living at the villa. No one drank anything stronger than champagne and it was very gay and obviously a splendid place to write. There was going to be everything that a man needed to write except to be alone.

19

A Matter of Measurements

Once, much later, in the time after Zelda had what was then called her first nervous breakdown and we happened to be in Paris at the same time, Scott asked me to have lunch with him at Michaud's restaurant on the corner of the rue Jacob and the rue des Saints-Pères. He said he had something very important to ask me that meant more than anything in the world to him and that I must answer him absolutely truly. I said that I would do the best that I could. For a long time, when he would ask me to tell him something absolutely truly, which is very difficult to do, and I would try it, the thing that I would say would make him angry; often not when I said it but afterwards, and sometimes long afterwards when he had brooded on it and it would be something that would have to be destroyed and sometimes, if possible, me with it.

He drank wine at the lunch but it did not affect him and he had not prepared for the lunch by drinking before it. We talked about our work and about people and he asked me about people that we had been out of touch with. I knew that he was writing something good and that he was having great trouble with it for many reasons but that was not what he wanted to talk about. I kept waiting for it to come, the thing that I had to tell the absolute truth about; but he would not bring it up until the end of the meal, as though we were having a business lunch.

Finally when we were eating the cherry tart and had a last carafe of wine he said, "You know I never slept with anyone except Zelda."

"No, I didn't."

"I thought I had told you."

"No. You told me a lot of things but not that."

"That is what I have to ask you about."

"Good. Go on."

"Zelda said that the way I was built I could never make any woman happy and that was what upset her originally. She said it was a matter of measurements. I have never felt the same since she said that and I have to know truly."

"Come out to the office," I said. "Or you go out first."

"Where is the office?"

"*Le water*," I said.

We came back into the room and sat down at the table.

"You're perfectly fine," I said. "You are O.K. There's nothing wrong with you. You look at yourself from above and you look foreshortened. Go over to the Louvre and look at the people in the statues then go home and look at yourself in the mirror in profile."

"Those statues may not be accurate."

"They are pretty good. Most people would settle for them."

"But why would she say it?"

"To put you out of business. That's the oldest way of putting people out of business in the world. Scott, you asked me to tell you the truth and I can tell you a lot more but this is the absolute truth and all you need. You could have gone to see a doctor."

"I didn't want to. I wanted you to tell me truly."

"Now do you believe me?"

"I don't know," he said.

"Come on over to the Louvre," I said. "It's just down the street and across the river."

We went over to the Louvre and he looked at the statues but still he was doubtful about himself.

"It is not basically a question of the size in repose," I said. "It is the size that it becomes. It is also a question of angle." I explained to him about using a pillow and a few other things that might be useful for him to know.

"There is one girl," he said, "who has been very nice to me. But after what Zelda said—"

"Forget what Zelda said," I told him. "Zelda is crazy. There's nothing wrong with you. Just have confidence and do what the girl wants. Zelda just wants to destroy you."

"You don't know anything about Zelda."

"All right," I said. "Let it go at that. But you came to lunch to ask me a question and I've tried to give you an honest answer."

But he was still doubtful.

"Should we go and see some pictures?" I asked. "Have you ever seen anything in here except the Mona Lisa?"

"I'm not in the mood for looking at pictures," he said. "I promised to meet some people at the Ritz bar."

Many years later at the Ritz bar, long after the end of World War II, Georges, who is the bar man now and who was the *chasseur* when Scott lived in Paris, asked me, "Papa, who was this Monsieur Fitzgerald that everyone asks me about?"

"Didn't you know him?"

"No. I remember all of the people of that time. But now they ask me only about him."

"What do you tell them?"

"Anything interesting that they wish to hear. What will please them. What do you wish? But tell me, who was he?"

"He was an American writer of the early Twenties and later who lived some time in Paris and abroad."

"But why would I not remember him? Was he a good writer?"

"He wrote two very good books and one which was not completed which those who know his writing best say would have been very good. He also wrote some good short stories."

"Did he frequent the bar much?"

"I believe so."

"But you did not come to the bar in the early Twenties. I know that you were poor then and lived in a different quarter."

"When I had money I went to the Crillon."

"I know that too. I remember very well when we first met."

"So do I."

"It is strange that I have no memory of him," Georges said.

"All those people are dead."

"Still one does not forget people because they are dead and people keep asking me about him. You must tell me something about him for my memoirs."

"I will."

"I remember you and the Baron von Blixen arriving one night—in what year?" He smiled.

"He is dead too."

"Yes. But one does not forget him. You see what I mean?"

"His first wife wrote very beautifully," I said. "She wrote perhaps the best book about Africa that I ever read. Except Sir Samuel Baker's book on the Nile tributaries of Abyssinia. Put that in your memoirs. Since you are interested in writers now."

"Good," said Georges. "The Baron was not a man that you forget. And the name of the book?"

"*Out of Africa,*" I said. "Blickie was always very proud of his first wife's writing. But we knew each other long before she had written that book."

"But Monsieur Fitzgerald that they keep asking me about?"

"He was in Frank's time."

"Yes. But I was the *chasseur.* You know what a *chasseur* is."

"I am going to write something about him in a book that I will write about the early days in Paris. I promised myself that I would write it."

"Good," said Georges.

"I will put him in exactly as I remember him the first time that I met him."

"Good," said Georges. "Then, if he came here, I will remember him. After all one does not forget people."

"Tourists?"

"Naturally. But you say he came here very much?"

"It meant very much to him."

"You write about him as you remember him and then if he came here I will remember him."

"We will see," I said.

ADDITIONAL PARIS SKETCHES

Birth of A New School

The blue-backed notebooks, the two pencils and the pencil sharpener (a pocket knife was too wasteful), the marble-topped tables, the smell of *café crèmes,* the smell of early morning sweeping out and mopping and luck were all you needed. For luck you carried a horse chestnut and a rabbit's foot in your right pocket. The fur had been worn off the rabbit's foot long ago and the bones and the sinews were polished by wear. The claws scratched in the lining of your pocket and you knew your luck was still there.

Some days it went so well that you could make the country so that you could walk into it through the timber to come out into the clearing and onto the high ground and see the hills beyond the arm of the lake. A pencil-lead might break off in the conical nose of the pencil sharpener and you would use the small blade of the pen knife to clear it or else sharpen the pencil carefully with the sharp blade and then slip your arm through the sweat-salted leather of your pack strap to lift the pack again, get the other arm through and feel the weight settle on your back and feel the pine needles under your moccasins as you started down for the lake.

Then you would hear someone say, "Hi, Hem. What are you trying to do? Write in a café?"

Your luck had run out and you shut the notebook. This was the worst thing that could happen. If you could keep your temper it would be better but I was not good at keeping mine then and said, "You rotten son of a bitch what are you doing in here off your filthy beat?"

"Don't be insulting just because you want to act like an eccentric."

"Take your dirty camping mouth out of here."

"It's a public café. I've just as much right here as you have."

"Why don't you go up to the Petite Chaumière where you belong?"

"Oh dear. Don't be so tiresome."

Now you could get out and hope it was an accidental visit and that the visitor had only come in by chance and there was not going to be an infestation. There were other good cafés to work in but they were a long walk away and this was your home café. It was bad to be driven out of the Closerie des Lilas. You had to make a stand or move. It was probably wiser to move but the anger started to come and I said, "Listen. A bitch like you has plenty of places to go. Why do you have to come here and louse a decent café?"

"I just came in to have a drink. What's wrong with that?"

"At home they'd serve you and then break the glass."

"Where's home? It sounds like a charming place."

He was sitting at the next table, a tall fat young man with spectacles. He had ordered a beer. I thought I would ignore him and see if I could write. So I ignored him and wrote two sentences.

"All I did was speak to you."

I went on and wrote another sentence. It dies hard when it is really going and you are into it.

"I suppose you've gotten so great nobody can speak to you."

I wrote another sentence that ended the paragraph and read it over. It was still all right and I wrote the first sentence of the next paragraph.

"You never think about anyone else or that they may have problems too."

I had heard complaining all my life. I found I could go on writing and that it was no worse than other noises; certainly better than Ezra learning to play the bassoon.

"Suppose you wanted to be a writer and feel it in every part of your body and it just wouldn't come."

I went on writing and I was beginning to have luck now as well as the other thing.

"Suppose once it had come like an irresistible torrent and then it left you mute and silent."

Better than mute and noisy, I thought, and went on writing. He was in full cry now and the unbelievable sentences were soothing as the noise of a plank being violated in the sawmill.

"We went to Greece," I heard him say later. I had not heard him for some time except as noise. I was ahead now and I could leave it and go on tomorrow.

"You say you used it or you went there?"

"Don't be vulgar," he said. "Don't you want me to tell you the rest?"

"No," I said. I closed the notebook and put it in my pocket.

"Don't you care how it came out?"

"No."

"Don't you care about life and the suffering of a fellow human being?"

"Not you."

"You're beastly."

"Yes."

"I thought you could help me, Hem."

"I'd be glad to shoot you."

"Would you?"

"No. There's a law against it."

"I'd do anything for you."

"Would you?"

"Of course I would."

"Then keep the muck away from this café. Start with that."

I stood up and the waiter came over and I paid.

"Can I walk down to the sawmill with you, Hem?"

"No."

"Well I'll see you some other time."

"Not here."

"That's perfectly right," he said. "I promised."*

"I have to write."

"I have to write too."

"You shouldn't write if you can't write. What do you have to cry about it for? Go home. Get a job. Hang yourself. Only don't talk about it. You could never write."

"Why do you say that?"

"Did you ever hear yourself talk?"

"It's writing I'm talking about."

"Then shut up."

"You're just cruel," he said. "Everybody always said you were cruel and heartless and conceited. I always defended you. But not any more."

"Good."

"How can you be so cruel to a fellow human being?"

"I don't know," I said. "Look, if you can't write why don't you learn to write criticism?"

"Do you think I should?"

"It would be fine," I told him. "Then you can always write. You won't ever have to worry about it not coming nor being mute and silent. People will read it and respect it."

"Do you think I could be a good critic?"

"I don't know how good. But you could be a critic. There will always be people who will help you and you can help your own people."

"What do you mean my own people?"

"The ones you go around with."

"Oh them. They have their critics."

"You don't have to criticize books," I said. "There's pictures, plays, ballet, the cinema—"

"You make it sound fascinating, Hem. Thank you so much. It's so exciting. It's creative too."

"Creation's probably overrated. After all, God made the world in only six days and rested on the seventh."

"Of course there's nothing to prevent me doing creative writing too."

"Not a thing. Except you may set yourself impossibly high standards by your criticism."

"They'll be high. You can count on that."

"I'm sure they will be."

He was a critic already so I asked him if he would have a drink and he accepted.

"Hem," he said, and I knew he was a critic now since, in conversation, they put your name at the beginning of a sentence rather than at the end, "I have to tell you I find your work just a little too stark."

"Too bad," I said.

"Hem it's too stripped, too lean."

"Bad luck."

"Hem too stark, too stripped, too lean, too sinewy."

I felt the rabbit's foot in my pocket guiltily. "I'll try to fatten it up a little."

"Mind, I don't want it obese."

"Harold," I said, practicing speaking like a critic, "I'll avoid that as long as I can."

"Glad we see eye to eye," he said manfully.

"You'll remember about not coming here when I'm working?"

"Naturally, Hem. Of course. I'll have my own café now."

"You're very kind."

"I try to be," he said.

It would be interesting and instructive if the young man had turned out to be a famous critic but it did not turn out that way although I had high hopes for a while.

*ALTERNATE ENDING:

I did not think that he would come back. The Closerie was off his beat and he had probably been passing and seen me working and come in. Or maybe he had come in to telephone. I would not have noticed while I was working. Poor bastard I thought but if I had been civil to him or decent even it would have been worse. I would have to hit him sooner or later probably but I would choose the place. I was damned if I would hit him at my home café and then have the others all coming to see the place where it happened. Sooner or later I would have to do it but I must be careful not to break the jaw. The hell with being careful of that, what I must be careful of was not to have his head hit on pavement. That was what you always think about. Keep out of the poor bastard's way I thought. Quit thinking about cooling people. You worked all right. He didn't do you any harm. If you run into him and he crowds you tell him to muck off. You were bad enough to him the way it was. But what other way could you be?

It was your own fault if anyone interfered with your working in a café because you had a good café for working where no one you knew would ever go. But the Closerie de Lilas was such a fine place to write and so convenient that it was worth the risk of being bothered. You ought to feel clean after you worked instead of dirtied though. Sure. And you ought not to have to be ruthless. Sure. But all that really mattered was that you go good the next day.

So the next day I woke early, boiled the rubber nipples and the bottles, made the formula, finished the bottling, gave Mr. Bumby a bottle and worked on the dining room table before anyone but he, F. Puss the cat, and I were awake. The two of them were quiet and good company and I worked better than I had ever done. In those days you did not really need anything, not even the rabbit's foot, but it was good to feel it in your pocket.

Ezra Pound and His Bel Esprit

Ezra Pound was the most generous writer I have ever known and the most disinterested. He was always doing something practical for poets, painters, sculptors and prose writers that he believed in and he would help anyone, whether he believed in them or not, if they were in trouble. He worried about everyone and in the time when I first knew him he was most worried about T. S. Eliot who, Ezra told me, had to work in a bank in London and so had insufficient time and bad hours to function as a poet.

Ezra founded something called Bel Esprit with Miss Natalie Barney who was a rich American woman and a patroness of the arts. Miss Barney had been a friend of Rémy de Gourmont who was before my time and she had a salon at her house on regular dates and a small Greek temple in her garden. Many American and French women with money enough had salons and I figured very early that they were excellent places for me to stay away from, but Miss Barney, I believe, was the only one that had a small Greek temple in her garden.

Ezra showed me the brochure for Bel Esprit and Miss Barney had allowed him to use the small Greek temple on the brochure. The idea of Bel Esprit was that we would all contribute a part of whatever we earned to provide a fund to get Mr. Eliot out of the bank so he would have money to write poetry. This seemed like a good idea to me and after we had got Mr. Eliot out of the bank Ezra figured we would go right straight along and fix up everybody.

I mixed things up a little by always referring to Eliot as Major Eliot pretending to confuse him with Major Douglas an economist about whose ideas Ezra was very enthusiastic. But Ezra understood that my heart was in the right place and that I was full of Bel Esprit even though it would annoy Ezra when I would solicit funds from my friends to get Major Eliot out of the bank and someone would say what was a Major doing in a bank anyway and if he had been axed by the military establishment did he not have a pension or at least some gratuity?

In such cases I would explain to my friends that this was all beside the point. Either you had Bel Esprit or you did not have it. If you had it you would subscribe to get the Major out of the bank. If you didn't it was too bad. Didn't they understand the significance of the small Greek temple? No? I thought so. Too bad, Mac. Keep your money. We wouldn't touch it.

As a member of Bel Esprit I campaigned energetically and my happiest dreams in those days were of seeing the Major stride out of the bank a free man. I cannot remember how Bel Esprit finally cracked up but I think it had something to do with the publication of *The Waste Land* which won the Major the Dial award and not long after a lady of title backed a review for Eliot called *The Criterion* and Ezra and I did not have to worry about him any more. The small Greek temple is, I believe, still in the garden. It was always a disappointment to me that we had not been able to get the Major out of the bank by Bel Esprit alone, as in my dreams I had pictured him as coming, perhaps, to live in the small Greek temple and that maybe I could go with Ezra when we would drop in to crown him with laurel. I knew where there was fine laurel that I could ride out and get on my bicycle and I thought we could crown him any time he felt lonesome or any time Ezra had gone over the manuscript or the proofs of another big poem like *The Waste Land*. The whole thing turned out badly for me morally, as so many things have, because the money that I had earmarked for getting the Major out of the bank I took out to Enghien and bet on jumping horses that raced under the influence of stimulants. At two meetings the stimulated horses that I was backing outraced the unstimulated or insufficiently stimulated beasts except for one race in which our fancy had been overstimulated to such a point that before the start he threw his jockey and breaking away completed a full circuit of the steeplechase course jumping beautifully by himself the way one can sometimes jump in dreams. Caught up and remounted he started the race and figured honorably, as the French racing phrase has it, but was out of the money.

I would have been happier if the amount of the wager had gone to Bel Esprit which was no longer existent. But I comforted myself that with those wagers which had prospered I could have contributed much more to Bel Esprit than was my original intention. It turned out all right though as we used the money to go to Spain.

On Writing in the First Person

When you first start writing stories in the first person, if the stories are made so real that people believe them, the people reading them nearly always think the stories really happened to you. That is natural because while you were making them up you had to make them happen to the person who was telling them. If you do this successfully enough, you make the person who is reading them believe that the things happened to him too. If you can do this you are beginning to get what you are trying for, which is to make something that will become a part of the reader's experience and a part of his memory. There must be things that he did not notice when he read the story or the novel which, without his knowing it, enter into his memory and experience so that they are a part of his life. This is not easy to do.

What is, if not easy, almost always possible to do is for members of the private detective school of literary criticism to prove that the writer of fiction written in the first person could not possibly have done everything that the narrator did or, perhaps, not even any of it. What importance this has or what it proves except that the writer is not devoid of imagination or the power of invention I have never understood.

In the early days writing in Paris I would invent not only from my own experience but from the experiences and knowledge of my friends and all the people I had known, or met since I could remember, who were not writers. I was very lucky always that my best friends were not writers and to have known many intelligent people who were articulate. In Italy when I was at the war there, for one thing that I had seen or that had happened to me, I knew many hundreds of things that had happened to other people who had been in the war in all of its phases. My own small experiences gave me a touchstone by which I could tell whether stories were true or false and being wounded was a password. After the war I spent much time in the 19th Ward and other Italian quarters in Chicago with an Italian friend I had made while in hospital in Milano. He was a young officer then and had been severely wounded many times. He had gone from Seattle, I think, to Italy to visit family there and had volunteered when Italy came into the war. We were very good friends and he was a wonderful storyteller.

In Italy too I had known many people in the British army and in their ambulance service. Much that I later invented from in writing I learned from them. My best friend for many years was a young British professional soldier who had gone from Sandhurst to Mons in 1914 and who had served with troops until the end of the war in 1918.

Secret Pleasures

As long as I did newspaper work and had to go to different parts of Europe on assignments it was necessary to have one presentable suit, go to the barber, and have one pair of respectable shoes. These were a liability when I was trying to write because they made it possible to leave your own side of the river and go over to the right bank to see your friends there, go to the races and do all the things that were fun that you could not afford or that got you into trouble. I found out very quickly that the best way to avoid going over to the right bank and get involved in all the pleasant things that I could not afford and that left me with, at least, gastric remorse was not to get a haircut. You could not go over to the right bank with your hair cut like one of those wonderful looking Japanese noblemen painters who were friends of Ezra's. That would have been ideal and would have limited you to your own side of the river completely and kept you working. You were never free of assignments long enough for that sort of mane to grow but in two months you would look like something left over from the American Civil War and unacceptable. After three months you would have a good start on the sort of hair cut Ezra's wonderful Japanese friends had and your right bank friends would think of you as damned. I never knew just what it was that you were supposed to be damned to but after four months or so you were considered damned to something worse. I enjoyed being considered damned and my wife and I enjoyed being considered damned together.

Sometimes I would run into foreign correspondents I knew when they were slumming in what they thought of as the Quarter and one would take me aside and talk to me seriously for my own good.

"You mustn't let yourself go, Hem. It's none of my business of course. But you can't go native this way. For God's sake straighten out and get a proper haircut at least."

Then if I was ordered to some conference or to Germany or the Near East I would have to get a haircut and wear my one passable suit and my good English shoes and sooner or later I would meet the man who had straightened me out and he'd say, "You're looking fit old boy. Dropped that bohemian nonsense I see. What are you up to tonight? There is a very good place, absolutely special, up beyond Taxim's."

People who interfered in your life always did it for your own good and I figured it out finally that what they wanted was for you to conform completely and never differ from some accepted surface standard and then dissipate the way traveling salesmen would at a convention in every stupid and boreing way there was. They knew nothing of our pleasures nor how much fun it was to be damned to ourselves and never would know nor could know. Our pleasures, which were those of being in love, were as simple and still as mysterious and complicated as a simple mathematical formula that can mean all happiness or can mean the end of the world.

That is the sort of happiness you should not tinker with but nearly everyone you knew tried to adjust it. Once we were back from Canada where I had decided that I would do no more newspaper work even if I starved and we lived as savages and kept our own tribal rules and had our own customs and our own standards, secrets, taboos and delights.*

We were free people now in Paris and I did not have to go on assignments.

"And I'm never going to get a haircut," I said while we were talking together at the Closerie des Lilas inside at a table where it was warm.

"Not if you don't want, Tatie."

"I started before we left Toronto."

"That's wonderful. That's a month anyway."

"Six weeks."

"Should we have a Chambéry Cassis to celebrate."

I ordered them and said, "Will you like it again?"

"Yes. It's part of being free from all that awfulness. Tell me how it will be."

"Do you remember the three Japanese painters at Ezra's?"

"Oh yes, Tatie, they were beautiful but that would take an awfully long time."

---

*The following fragment was crossed out: "We had been armoured together by two things. The first was the loss of everything I had written over a period of four years except for two stories and a few poems. I was working at the Lausanne conference for the *Toronto Star* and two news services the International and Universal. Before Christmas I had arranged for someone to fill in for me for the news-services and had written Hadley to come down so we could go skiing together over the holidays. It had been an interesting conference and I had been working very hard running a twenty four hour service for the two agencies under two different by-lines, my own and an imaginary character named John Hadley who was supposed to be a middle aged and un-impeachable authority on European politics. My last dispatch would be filed sometime before three o'clock in the morning and I would leave a wire opener for the morning with the concierge at the desk when I went up to bed.

The morning Hadley's train was to get in I went down to go to the station to meet her and the concierge gave me a cable. She was coming on a later train."

"That was the way I always wanted it."

"We can try. It grows awfully fast. "

"I wish I could start it that way tomorrow."

"There isn't any way, Tatie, except just for it to grow. You know that. It takes such a long time. I'm sorry it does."*

"Damn it."

"Let me feel."

"Here?"

"It's growing wonderfully. You'll just have to be patient."

"All right. I'll forget about it."

"If you don't think about it maybe it will grow faster. I'm so glad you remembered to start it so early."

We looked at each other and laughed and then she said one of the secret things.

"That's correct."

"Tatie, I thought of something exciting."

"Tell me."

"I don't know whether to say it."

"Say it. Go on. Please say it."

"I thought maybe it could be the same as mine."

"But yours keeps on growing too."

"No. I'll get it just evened tomorrow and then I'll wait for you. Wouldn't that be fine for us?"

"Yes."

"I'll wait and then it will be the same for both."

"How long will it take?"

"Maybe four months to be just the same."

*The following fragment was removed here: "When we lived in Austria in the winter we would cut each other's hair and let it grow to the same length. One was dark and the other dark red gold and in the dark in the night one would wake the other swinging the heavy dark or the heavy silken red gold across the others lips in the cold dark in the warmth of the bed. You could see your breath if there was moonlight."

"Really?"

"Really."

"Four months more?"

"I think so."

We sat and she said something secret and I said something secret back.

"Other people would think we are crazy."

"Poor unfortunate other people," she said. "We'll have such fun, Tatie."

"And you'll really like it?"

"I'll love it," she said. "But we'll have to be very patient. The way people are patient with a garden."

"I'll be patient, or I'll try anyway."

"Do you think other people have such fun with such simple things?"

"Maybe it's not so simple."

"I don't know. Nothing can be simpler than growing."

"I don't care whether it's complicated or simple I just like it."

"So do I. We're awfully lucky aren't we? My I wish I could help but I don't know how we can make it faster."

"Do you think we could cut it across at the same length as yours? That would be a start."

"I'll do that if you want. It would be simpler than asking a barber to. But the rest would have to grow down to it, Tatie. It has to grow from the front all the way down to the back. The way we want it. That's what takes so long."

"Damn it taking so long."

"I'll think what we can do. But it has grown six weeks and now while we are here in the café too. It will certainly grow tonight."

"It certainly will."

"I'll think of something."

The next day she came home from the hairdressers and her hair was cut below her ears so it came below her cheek and swung against her neck and she turned and in the back it was about an inch above her sweater neck. It was new washed and rusty gold.

"Feel it in back," she said.

I put my arm around her and felt our hearts beating through our sweaters and I brought my right hand up and felt her neck smooth and the hair thick against it under my fingers that were shaking.

"Shake it down hard," she said.

"Wait," I said,

Then she said, "Now stroke it down hard. Feel."

I held my hand against the silky weight and bluntness against her neck and said something secret and she said, "Afterwards."

"You," I said. "You."

Afterwards we were talking and she said, "I thought something out and did something practical, Tatie. It's cut a whole inch shorter. Didn't you see? Couldn't you feel? Now you've gained a full inch. That's almost a month."

I could not say anything.

"Then in another week I'll have them cut it another inch shorter and it will still be the way you like it. You didn't even notice it was shorter did you?"

"No. It's wonderful."

"You see how intelligent I was? Then you'll have gained two months. I could go and get it done this afternoon but I might as well wait until I go to have it washed again."

"It's wonderful the way it is."

"I'll cut yours across now to make the line."

"Do you think we should?"

"Of course, Tatie. Wasn't that what we said?"

"It will look sort of funny maybe."

"Not to us. Who are the others anyway?"

"Nobody."

After I had sat on one of the dining room chairs with a towel around my neck and she had cut the line across the back the same distance above my sweater collar as the line where hers was cut and brushed back all the hair above the ears tight against my head and cut another line from the corner of the eyes to the upper base of the ear she said, "I was wrong, Tatie, about four months. It will probably be longer."

"Do you think so? In Toronto I didn't let them cut anything off the sides or the top for over a month before the last time. I just had the back trimmed six weeks ago."

"How can you remember all that?"

"It was as soon as I knew we were leaving. You remember those things like getting out of jail."

"That wasn't too late in the fall then. It's fine, Tatie. I just cut that line because that all has to grow so it will become down like mine does here. See," she pushed her hair up and behind her ear then let it drop forward, "that's where it starts. Yours grows thick there and it is long already. In a month you won't be able to keep it from coming over your ears. Are you getting frightened?"

"Maybe."

"I am a little bit too. But we're going to do it aren't we?" she said.

"Sure."

"I'm glad if you're glad."

"We really want to don't we?"

"Do we?"

"Yes."

"Then we'll do it."

"Are you sure?" I said.

"Yes."

"And nothing anybody says will make any difference?"

"Nothing."

"Of course we've been doing it since yesterday."

"And you since Toronto."

"No. This other."

"We'll just do it and not worry and have a lovely time. Are you happy now that we've really started and done something practical?"

"I'm proud of you for thinking it out." I said.

"Now we have another secret. We won't say anything to anybody."

"Never. How long will we do it for?"

"A year?"

"No for six months."

"We'll see."

That was one of the years we went to Austria for the winter. There in Schruns nobody cared how you dressed nor how your hair was cut except that since we came from Paris some people in Schruns thought that it must be the style there. It had been the style once and so it probably was the style again.

Herr Nels, the hotel keeper who wore an imperial in the style of Napoleon III, and who had lived in Lorraine, told me he remembered when all men wore their hair long and that it was only the Prussians who had their hair cropped short. He said he was very pleased that Paris was again returning to this fashion. At the barber shop where I went the barber was very particular to try and get the fashion correct and took a great interest. He had seen it in Italian illustrated papers, he said. Not everyone could wear it, he said, but he was glad to see it coming back. He thought it was a revolt against the years of war. A sound and good thing.

Later he told me several of the other young men of the village were having their hair cut in the same style although it did not show to any great advantage yet. Could he ask how long mine had been growing?

"About three months."

"Then they must be patient. They all wish it to grow below the ears over night."

"It takes patience," I said.

"And when will yours be the length the mode requires?"

"In six months, who knows exactly?"

"I have an herbal preparation that has had a great success. It is a magnificent stimulant. Would you try a *friction* with it?"

"How does it smell?"

"It has only the odor of herbs. It is pleasant."

So I had the herbal tonic which smelled very herbal and when I stopped at the wine steube I noticed that the others of the younger and wilder wine steube set smelled the same.

"So he sold it to you too," Hans said.

"Yes. Does it do any good?"

"He says so. Did you buy a bottle too?"

"Yes."

"We're damned fools," Hans said. "To spend money to make our hair grow so we can have it cut the way it was when we were boys. Tell me. Is it really the style in Paris?"

"No."

"I'm glad. Why do you cut yours that way?"

"For fun."

"Good. Me too then. But we won't tell the barber."

"No, nor the others."

"No. Tell me does your wife like it?"

"Yes."

"My girl too."

"Did she ask you to do it?"

"No. We both spoke of it."

"It takes a long time though."

"We must be patient."

So we had one more thing that was a pleasure that winter.

A Strange Fight Club

Larry Gains was a tall, long muscled Negro heavyweight with a nice un-marked face and good manners who came to Paris from Canada where he had been the amateur champion. In Paris someone steered him into the hands of a manager named Anastasie who had a stable of fighters and this manager billed him at once as the heavyweight champion of Canada. The real heavyweight champion of Canada was a seasoned professional named Jack Renault who knew all the moves and hit hard with both hands and Larry Gains could not have remained upright in the same ring with him for long.

My wife and I had been away from Paris on a trip and when we came back to the flat over the Bal Musette at the top of the rue Cardinal Lemoine in shucking through the mail looking for checks I found a letter from Lou Marsh who was the sports editor on the Toronto Star asking me to look after Larry and a note from Larry giving me his address. In the morning sporting paper *L'Auto* there was an article about Larry Gains the Canadian heavyweight champion who was making his first fight in France on the following Saturday at the Stade Anastasie in the rue Pelleport on Ménilmontant the next tough hill of Paris to your right past the Buttes Chaumont if you should be standing in the middle of the slaughter house quarter looking towards the Porte de la Villette. An easier way to figure it was that it was the next to the last station on the Metro line that ran to the Porte des Lilas just before the reservoir of Ménilmontant. It was a very tough neighborhood, had good communications and would draw from three of the toughest quarters in Paris including Belleville. It was close enough to draw from Père Lachaise cemetery if any of the dead had been fight fans.

I sent a pneumatique to Larry and we met at the Café Napolitain on the Boulevard des Italiens. Larry was a very nice boy and sitting at the table with him the first thing I noticed beside his un-marked face, his general build and his good manners were his strange long hands. He had the longest hands I had ever seen on a boxer. They would not fit into any ordinary boxing glove and on his way to France he had one fight in England with a middleweight named Frank Moody who came in at catch weights.

"He beat me Mr. Ernest," Larry said. "Because the gloves were too short for my hands. My hands were cramped up so tight they were useless to me."

Frank Moody was then quite a good fighter and after I had seen Larry work I could think of several reasons why Frank Moody could have beaten him even if his gloves had fitted. We went up on the metro to the tough hill that the rue Pelleport climbed and I found that the Stade Anastasie was a sort of dance hall restaurant with a few rooms over the restaurant in a wooded vacant lot with a wall around it. A ring had been set up under the trees where the fighters worked out in good weather and there was a heavy bag and a light bag and mats in the dance hall. They could rig a ring there too in bad weather.

Saturday nights in late spring, summer and early fall there would be fights in the outdoor ring with rows of numbered chairs set up around the ring. The clients dined first at the restaurant and at the tables set up in the dance hall where the fighters, who ate and lived at the place unless they were local boys, served as the waiters. You could buy numbered seats at the entrance or you could buy an entrée which entitled you to enter the grounds where you could eat and drink at the restaurant and then stand to watch the fights. The prices were low and the food was excellent.

The first day at the Stade Anastasie I did not know all this. I had only been told it. What I knew was that it was a healthy part of Paris to live and work out in at this time of year. I could see that Larry stripped light for a heavy weight. He had a big frame and good long muscles but he had not filled out yet and was really an over grown boy but knew nothing. Larry had a long reach, a good left jab and a nice straight right and he was very light on his feet and moved very fast. He had wonderful legs and he moved faster and further and more uselessly than any heavyweight I had ever seen. He was a true amateur. After he had stuck and stabbed and danced after the harmless heavyweight for a while varying this with quick classic flights while the heavyweight stalked him with nothing Anastasie's trainer put a welterweight from Marseilles who was growing into a middleweight in with him. This boy moved in under the jab which did not go down as well as it went straight out and commenced to crack Larry in the body and Larry grabbed him. It was pitiful. Suddenly Larry's arms were too long, there was no place for him to dance to and the boy was inside of him anytime he wanted to be with both hands to the body and Larry knew nothing except to grab.

"Who is he fighting on Saturday?" I asked the trainer.

"Don't worry," he said.

"Any heavyweight will murder him."

"Not here."

"You'd better take the corners out of the ring."

"I give him back his confidence," the trainer said and called time and motioned for a new heavyweight who had just come over from the restaurant side.

Larry was walking around the ring taking deep breaths. The welterweight had the gloves off and was shadow boxing around the ring snorting through his nose his chin down on his chest. Larry watched him warily as he himself walked still breathing deeply. Look after him, Lou Marsh had written in the letter. This is the damndest place I've ever seen I thought. Look after him.

"Aren't you going to show him how to protect himself in close?" I asked the trainer. "He's going to fight on Saturday."

"Too late," the trainer said. "I'm not going to ruin his style."

"His style?"

"He has a *jeux des jambes fantastiques,*" the trainer said. "*Tu ne sais pas vu?*"

He was telling me that he could not risk spoiling Larry's fantastic footwork.

The new heavy weight was a local boy who had been employed carrying parts of carcasses in the stockyards until he had an accident which affected his reasoning power.

"He doesn't know his own strength," the trainer told me. "He has only rudimentary notions of *la boxe.* But he is very obedient."

The trainer gave him his orders before he got into the ring, an effort which seemed complicated for him. The orders were simple, "Cover up." The carcass carrier nodded and bit his lower lip in concentration. When he was safely in the ring the trainer repeated, "Cover up." Then the trainer added, "Don't bite your lower lip." The carrier nodded and the trainer called time.

The carcass man placed his two hands in front of his face

with the gloves almost touching. His elbows were tight against his body and his chin was down on his chest tucked behind his left shoulder which was raised painfully. He plodded slowly toward Larry his left foot moving forward and his right dragging up to it.

Larry stopped him with a jab, jabbed again, and threw a right that went in on the c.m.'s forehead. The carcass man thought heavily and began to move backwards slowly, the left foot retreating carefully and the right being slowly but precisely brought up to it. Larry now turned on all his beautiful footwork at once and stalked the c.m. like a prancing puma, his jab flicking out, his right poised.

"Your left," the trainer called to the c.m. "Jab your left."

Slowly the carcass man detached the left glove from the side of his head and rabidly extended it toward Larry who settled in his superb footwork long enough to paste the c.m. with a nice right hand on the mouth.

"See how he covers his jaw with the shoulder?" The trainer asked me.

"What about his belly."

"Larry doesn't hit to the belly," the trainer said.

I thought I might as well learn the worst.

"Hook him in the belly, Larry," I said. "And bring his hands down."

Larry danced on in beautifully, dropped his left hand so he was dead to a right hand puncher, and any heavyweight on earth has a right hand, and swung his left hand into the carcass man's belly. The c.m. sunk in on himself but his hands stayed up.

"What do you want to do?" the trainer asked me. "Change his style?"

"*Merde*," I said.

"He has a fight on Saturday. Do you want him to break

his hands on the boy's elbows? Do you want to ruin him? I'm in charge of him. You're not in charge of him. Shut up."

I shut up and watched Larry dance and peck a hole open between the two raised gloves, circle and land straight rights to the c.m.'s left ear, to the forehead and another nice one to the mouth when the c.m. jabbed again on demand. At least he punched straight and he did move around but I kept thinking about Jack Renault who was the real heavyweight champion of Canada and of all the things that Larry had to learn.

The boy Larry fought in his first fight in Paris did not know much more than the carcass man but he wanted to fight and did not keep covered up. Larry jabbed him and jabbed him. The jabs were solid and they hurt and they cut. The other heavyweight had a hungry look and was just out of the army and Larry moved around him so fast jabbing him that the crowd was crazy about it. Larry hit him with a really good but long right that shook the other boy and as he started to go Larry forgot all he knew and started swinging and never stopped until the boy slipped off the ropes and fell head first down onto the canvas.

After the fight Larry said, "I'm sorry. Tell your wife too I'm sorry please. I know I didn't look good but I'll be better next time."

"They thought you looked wonderful. The crowd was crazy about it."

"Oh sure," Larry said. "Could I see you Monday maybe to talk about the fight and things?"

"Sure. At the same café, the Napolitain, at noon."

The Stade Anastasie had turned out to be a very strange fight club.

The Acrid Smell of Lies

*Ford: He sat upright like a great gasping fish breathing out
a fouler breath than the spout of any whale.*

Many people loved Ford. Most of them, of course, were
women. But a few men liked him after they knew him and
many men tried to be just to him all of their lives. These
were people who, like H.G. Wells, had seen him in a good
époque and had seen him badly treated.

I never knew him in a good époque although his *Transatlantic Review* period was very well spoken of both at the
time and later. Almost everyone lies and the lies are not
important. Some people we loved for their lies and would
wait hopefully for them to start their best ones. Ford, though,
lied about things that left scars. He lied about money and
about things that were important in daily living that he
would give you his word on. When his luck was running very
badly he would sometimes give you close to a straight
answer. If he made any money or his luck turned for the better he became impossible. I tried to be just to him and not be
severe, nor judge him, but only try to get along with him; but
to think or write about him with accuracy and exactitude
was crueler than any judging.

After I had met Ford first in Ezra's studio when my wife
and I had come back from Canada with a six month old
child and found the saw mill apartment on the same street

where Ezra lived on, and moved into it in the dead of winter, Ezra told me I must be kind to Ford and I must not mind him lying.

"He always lies when he is tired, Hem," Ezra told me. "The way he was tonight wasn't bad at all. You should understand that he lies when he is tired. One night he was very tired and he told me a very long story about crossing the south west part of the United States in the early days with a puma."

"Was he ever in the south west?"

"Of course not. That's not the point, Hem. He was tired."

Ezra told me how Ford, unable to get a divorce from his first wife, when he was Ford Madox Hueffer, had gone to Germany where he had relatives. There it seems he had stayed until he convinced himself that he had become a German citizen and had obtained a valid German divorce. On his return to England his first wife had not agreed to this solution and Ford had found himself cruelly persecuted and many of his friends had behaved shabbily towards him. There was much more to it than this and it was more complicated and had many interesting people in it, all of whom are much less interesting now. Any man who had been able to convince himself that he had a divorce, and then was persecuted for such a simple error, deserved sympathy of a kind, and I wanted to ask Ezra if Ford had been tired during all that period; but I was sure he must have been.

"Was that why he changed his name from Hueffer?" I asked.

"There were many reasons. He changed it after the war."

Ford had started the *Transatlantic Review*. He had once edited *The English Review* in London before the war and before his domestic trouble and Ezra told me this had been a really good review and Ford had done a splendid job of editing. Now under his new name, he was making a new start. There was a new Mrs. Ford, a very pleasant, dark, young Australian woman named Stella Bowen who was a serious painter and they had a young daughter named Julie, a large child for her age, who was very fair and had good manners. She was a good-looking child and Ford told me that she looked in features and in coloring almost as he had looked at her age.

I had a completely unreasonable physical antipathy to Ford which was not simply for his bad breath, although I found I could alleviate it by trying to always keep windward of him. He had another very distinct odor that had nothing to do with his breath that made it almost impossible for me to be in a closed room with him. This odor would increase when he was lying and it had a sweetly acrid quality. Maybe it was the odor that he gave off when he was tired. I tried always to see him in the open air if possible and when I would go down to Bill Bird's hand press on the Quai d'Anjou at the Ile St.-Louis where he edited his review to read manuscripts for him, I always took the manuscripts out of the shop and sat on the wall of the Quai under the shade of the big trees to read them. I would have read them out there anyway as it was pleasant on the Quai and the light was good but I always had to go out of the shop as soon as I could when Ford came in.

The Education of Mr. Bumby

My first son, Bumby, and I spent much time together in the
cafés where I worked when he was very young and we lived
over the saw mill. He always went with us to Schruns in the
Vorarlberg in the winters but when Hadley and I were in
Spain in the summers he would pass those months with the
femme de ménage who he called Marie Cocotte and her husband, who he called Touton, either at 10 bis Avenue de Gob-
elins where they had a flat or at Mur de Bretagne where
they went for monsieur Rohrbach's summer vacations. Monsieur Rohrbach had been a *maréchal de logis chef* or sergeant
major in the professional French military establishment and
on his retirement had a minor functional post on which they
had lived with his and Marie's wages and looked forward to
his retirement to Mur de Bretagne. Touton had a great part in
the formative years of Bumby's life and when there would be
too many people at the Closerie de Lilas for us to work well
or I thought he needed a change of scene I would wheel him
in his carriage or later we would walk to the café on the Place
St.-Michel where he would study the people and the busy life
of that part of Paris where I did my writing over a *café
crème*. Everyone had their private cafés there where they
never invited anyone and would go to work, or to read or to
receive their mail. They had other cafés where they would
meet their mistresses and almost everyone had another café,
a neutral café, where they might invite you to meet their

mistress and there were regular, convenient, cheap dining places where everyone might eat on neutral ground. It was nothing like the organization of the Montparnasse quarter centered about the Dome, Rotonde, Select and later the Coupole or the Dingo bar which you read about in the books of early Paris.

As Bumby grew to be a bigger boy he spoke excellent French and, while he was trained to keep absolutely quiet and only study and observe while I worked, when he saw that I was finished he would confide in me something that he had learned from Touton.

"*Tu sais, Papa, que les femmes pleurent comme les enfants pissent?*"

"Did Touton tell you that?"

"He says a man should never forget it."

At another time he would say, "Papa four *poules* passed while you were working that were not bad."

"What do you know about *poules*?"

"Nothing. I observe them. One observes them."

"What does Touton say about them?"

"One does not take them seriously."

"What does one take seriously?"

"*Vive la France et les pommes de terre frites.*"

"Touton is a great man," I said.

"And a great soldier," Bumby said. "He taught me much."

"I admire him very much," I said.

"He admires you too. He says you have a very difficult *métier*. Tell me Papa is it difficult to write?"

"Sometimes."

"Touton says it is very difficult and I must always respect it."

"You respect it."

"Papa have you lived much among the *Peau-Rouges*?"

"A little," I said.

"Should we go home by Silver Beach's book store?"

"Sure. Do you like her?"

"She is always very nice to me."

"Me too."

"She has a beautiful name. Silver Beach."

"We will go by and then I must get you home in time for lunch. I have promised to have lunch with some people."

"Interesting people?"

"People," I answered.

It was too early for them to be sailing boats in the Luxembourg gardens and so we did not stop to watch that and when we arrived home Hadley and I had quarreled about something in which she had been right and I had been wrong quite seriously.

"Mother has been bad. Papa has scolded her," Bumby announced in French very grandly still under the influence of Touton.

After Scott had taken to turning up drunk quite frequently Bumby asked me very seriously one morning when he and I had finished work together at the Place St.-Michel café, "Monsieur Fitzgerald is sick Papa?"

"He is sick because he drinks too much and he cannot work."

"Does he not respect his *métier*?"

"Madame his wife does not respect it or she is envious of it."

"He should scold her."

"It is not so simple."

"Are we meeting him today?"

"Yes, I believe so."

"Will he be drinking so much?"

"No. He said we would not be drinking."

"I will make an example."

That afternoon when Scott and I met with Bumby at a neutral café Scott was not drinking and we each ordered a bottle of mineral water.

"For me a *demi-blonde*," Bumby said.

"Do you allow that child to drink beer?" Scott asked.

"Touton says that a little beer does no harm to a boy of my age," Bumby said. "But make it a *ballon*."

A *ballon* was only a half glass of beer.

"Who is this Touton?" Scott asked me.

I told him about Touton and how he might have come out of the memoirs of Marbot or of Ney, if he had written his, and that he embodied the traditions of the orders of the old French military establishment which had been destroyed many times but still existed. Scott and I talked of the Napoleonic campaigns and the war of 1870 which he had not studied and I told him some stories of the mutinies in the French army after the Nivelle offensive at the Chemin des Dames that I had heard from friends who had participated in them and how such men as Touton were an anachronism but an absolutely valid thing. Scott was passionately interested in the war of 1914–18 and since I had many friends who had served in it and some who had seen many things in detail recently these stories of the war as it actually was were shocking to him. The talk was far over Bumby's head but he listened attentively and afterwards when we had talked of other things and Scott had left, full of mineral water and the resolve to write well and truly, I asked Bumby why he had ordered a beer.

"Touton says that a man should first learn to control himself," he said. "I thought I could make an example."

"It is not so simple as that," I told him.

"War is not simple either is it Papa?"

"No. Very complicated. You believe what Touton tells you now. Then later you will find out many things for yourself."

"Monsieur Fitzgerald was demolished mentally by the war? Touton told me many people were."

"No. He was not."

"I am glad," Bumby said. "It must be some passing thing."

"It would be no disgrace if he had been demolished mentally by the war," I said. "Many of our good friends were. Later some recovered to do fine things. Our friend André Masson the painter."

"Touton explained to me about it being no disgrace to be demolished mentally. There was too much artillery in this last war. And the generals were all *cows*."

"It is very complicated," I said. "You will find it all out some day for yourself."

"Meantime it is nice that we have no problems of our own. No grave problems. You worked well today?"

"Very well."

"I am happy," Bumby said. "If I can be helpful in anything?"

"You help me very much."

"Poor Monsieur Fitzgerald," Bumby said. "He was very nice today to remain sober and not molest you. Will everything be all right with him Papa?"

"I hope so," I said. "But he has very grave problems. It seems to me that he has almost insurmountable problems as a writer."

"I am sure that he will surmount them." Bumby said. "He was so very nice today and so reasonable."

Scott and His Parisian Chauffeur

After the Princeton game in the fall of 1928 Scott and Zelda, Henry (Mike) Strater, my wife Pauline and I rode in the crowded after football train to Philadelphia where we were to pick up the Fitzgerald's French chauffeur with their Buick car to drive to where they lived on the river outside Wilmington in a house called Ellerslie Mansion. Scott and Mike Strater had been at Princeton together and Mike and I had been good friends since we had first met in 1922 in Paris.

Scott took football very seriously and he had stayed sober through most of the game. But on the train he had started speaking to people he did not know and asking them questions. Several girls were annoyed by him but Mike or I would speak to their escorts and quiet any rising feeling and maneuver Scott away from trouble. We had him seated several times but he wanted to wander through the cars and he had been so reasonable and decent all day that I thought we could help keep him out of anything serious. We had no choice but to try to take care of him and as he realized that he was being taken out of trouble as soon as he started it he began to expand his operations alternating indiscrete questions with excessive courtliness while one of us gently moved him along and the other apologized.

Finally he found a Princeton supporter who was now absorbed in reading a medical book. Scott took the book away from him in a courtly way saying, "Do you mind Sir?"

glanced at it and returned it with a bow in a voice pitched for all that part of the car, "Ernest I have found a clap doctor!"

The man paid no attention to Scott and went on reading in his book.

"You are a clap doctor aren't you?" Scott asked him.

"Come on Scott cut it out," I said. Mike was shaking his head.

"Speak up Sir," Scott said. "There is nothing to be ashamed about being a clap doctor."

I was trying to work Scott away and Mike was speaking to the man apologizing for Scott. The man was keeping out of it and trying to study.

"A clap doctor," Scott said. "Physician heal thyself."

We got him away from persecuting the medical student finally and the train eventually came into the station at Philadelphia with no one having hit Scott. Zelda had been in one of her periods of perfect ladyhood on the train sitting quietly with Pauline and paying no attention to Scott's behavior.

The driver of the car was a Parisian taxi driver who neither spoke nor understood English. He had brought Scott home one night in Paris Scott told me and had kept him from being robbed. Scott had brought him to America as his chauffeur. As we drove toward Wilmington from Philadelphia in the dark with the drinking now started the chauffeur was worried because the car heated up.

"You should have filled the radiator," I said.

"No, Monsieur. It isn't that. Monsieur will not allow me to put any oil in the motor."

"How's that?"

"He gets very angry and says American cars don't need to have oil added. That only worthless French cars need additional oil."

"Why don't you ask Madame?"

"She gets even more angry."

"Do you want to stop and put in some oil now?"

"It could make a dreadful scene."

"Let's stop and put some in."

"No Monsieur. You don't know the scenes there have been."

"The motor's boiling now," I said.

"But if I stop to put gas and fill with water I must stop the engine. They will not put gas in without the engine being stopped, then the cold water will crack the cylinder block. There is plenty of water Monsieur. It is a very big cooling system."

"For Christ sake let's stop and put in water with the engine running."

"No Monsieur. I tell you Monsieur would never permit it. I know this motor. It will reach the chateau. This is not the first time. Tomorrow if you would come with me to a garage. We can go when I take the little girl to church."

"Sure," I said.

"We'll change the oil," he said. "We'll buy some tins. I'll keep them hidden and add them when it needs them."

"Are you jabbering about oil?" Scott said. "Philippe has some sort of fixation that you have to put oil in this car all the time like that ridiculous Renault we drove up from Lyon that time. *Philippe, écoute, voiture américain pas d'huile.*"

"*Oui Monsieur,*" the chauffeur said.

"He makes Zelda nervous with that silly oil chatter," Scott said. "He's a good fellow and absolutely loyal but he knows nothing about American motors."

It was a nightmare ride and when the driver wanted to turn off at the side road that led to the house Zelda would not let him. Both she and Scott insisted that it was not the road. Zelda claimed the turn off was much further on and Scott said we had passed it. They argued and quarreled until Zelda went to sleep momentarily while the chauffeur drove slowly on. Then Scott told the driver to turn around and while he was napping too the chauffeur made the turn off.

The Pilot Fish and the Rich

The first year in the Vorarlberg was an innocent year. The second year of the great killing by avalanches was a different kind of year and you began to know people and the places very well. You knew some people too well and you were learning the places for survival as well as for pleasure. The last year was a nightmare and a murder year disguised as the greatest fun of all. It was that year that the rich showed up.

The rich always have a sort of pilot fish who goes ahead of them, sometimes he is a little deaf, sometimes a little blind, but always smelling affably and hesitant ahead of them. The pilot fish talks like this: "Well I don't know. No of course not really. But I like them. I like them both. Yes, by God, Hem; I do like them. I see what you mean (giggle) but I do like them truly and there's something damned fine about her." (He gives her name and pronounces it lovingly.) "No, Hem, don't be silly and don't be difficult. I like them truly. Both of them I swear it. You'll like him (using his baby-talk nickname) when you know him. I like them both, truly."

Then you have the rich and nothing is ever as it was again. The pilot fish leaves of course. He is always going somewhere, or coming from somewhere, and he is never around for very long. He enters and leaves politics or the theater in the same way he enters and leaves countries and people's lives in his early days. He is never caught and he is not caught by the rich. Nothing ever catches him and it is only those who trust him who are caught and killed. He has the irreplaceable early training of the bastard and a latent and long denied love of money. He ends up rich himself, having moved one dollar's width to the right with every dollar that he made.

These rich loved and trusted him because he was shy, comic, elusive, already in production, and because he was an unerring pilot fish they could tell that through all the then true sincerity of his politics it was a passing sham and that he was one of them although he did not know it then.

When you have two people who love each other, are happy and gay and really good work is being done by one or both of them, people are drawn to them as surely as migrating birds are drawn at night to a powerful beacon. If the two people were as experienced or as solidly constructed as the beacon there would be little damage except to the birds. The people who attract people by their happiness and their performance are usually inexperienced but they learn quite rapidly how not to be overrun and they learn how to go away. But they have not learned about the good, the attractive, the charming, the soon-beloved, the generous, the understanding rich who have no bad qualities and who give each day the quality of a festival and who, when they have passed and taken the nourishment they needed, leave everything deader than the roots of any grass Attila's horses' hooves have ever scoured.

That year the rich came led by the pilot fish. A year before they would never have come. There was no certainty then. The work was as good and happiness was greater but no novel had been written, so they could not be sure. They never wasted their time nor their charm on something that was not sure. Why should they? Picasso was sure and of course had been before they had ever heard of painting. They were very sure of another painter. Many others. But this was the one they had taken up. He was a good enough painter too if you liked it and no one's fool. But this year they were sure and they had the word from the pilot fish who turned up too so we would not feel that they were outlanders and that I would not be difficult. The pilot fish was our friend of course.

It gives me the horrors now to remember it. In those days I trusted the pilot fish as I would trust, in those days, the Corrected Hydrographic Sailing Directions for the Mediterranean, say, or the tables in *Brown's Nautical Almanac*. Under the charm of these rich I was as trusting and as stupid as a bird dog who wants to go out with any man with a gun, or a trained pig in a circus who has finally found someone who loves and appreciates him for himself alone. That every day should be a fiesta seemed to me a wonderful discovery. I even read aloud the part of the novel that I had rewritten, which is about as low as a writer can get and much more dangerous for him as a writer than glacier skiing unroped before the full winter snowfall has set over the crevices.

When they said, "It's great, Ernest. Truly it's great. You cannot know the thing it has," I wagged my tail in pleasure and plunged into the every day a fiesta concept of life to see if I could not bring some fine attractive stick back, instead of thinking, "If these bastards like it what is wrong with it?" That was what I would think if I had been functioning as a professional although, if I had been functioning as a professional, I would never have read it to them.

That was a horror winter. Before these rich had come we had already been infiltrated by another rich using the oldest trick probably that there is. This is when an unmarried young woman becomes the temporary best friend of another young woman who is married, comes to live with the husband and wife and then unknowingly, innocently and unrelentingly sets out to marry the husband. When the husband is a writer and doing difficult work on a book so that he is occupied much of the time and is not a good companion or partner to his wife for a big part of the day, the arrangement has advantages until you know how it works out. The husband has two attractive girls around when he has finished work. One is new and strange and if he has bad luck he gets to love them both. Then the one who is relentless wins.

It sounds very silly. But to really love two women at the same time, truly love them, is the most destructive and terrible thing that can happen to a man when the unmarried one decides to marry. The wife does not know about it and trusts the husband. They have been through really difficult times and share those times and have loved each other and she finally trusts the husband truly and completely. The new one says you cannot really love her if you love your wife too. She does not say that at the start. That comes later when the murder's done. That comes when you lie to everyone all around and all you know is that you truly love two women. There is all that time when you do things that are impossible and when you are with one you love her and with the other you love her and together you love them both. You break all promises and you do everything you knew that you could never do nor would want to do. The one who is relentless wins. But finally it is the one who loses that wins and that is the luckiest thing that ever happened for me. So that was the sort of winter the last one was. These are the things I remember about it.

They have shared in everything, they are never bored together and they have something that is unbreakable. They love their child and they love Paris, Spain, parts of Switzerland, the Dolomites, and the Vorarlberg. They love their work and she has sacrificed hers to his and never mentioned it.

Then, instead of the two of them and their child, there are three of them. First it is wonderful and fun and it goes on that way for a while. All things to be truly wicked must start from an innocence. So you live day by day and enjoy what you have and do not worry. You love both and you lie and hate it and it destroys you and every day is more dangerous and you work harder and when you come out from your work you know what is happening is impossible, but you live day to day as in a war. Everyone is still happy except you when you wake in the middle of the night. You love them both now and you are gone. Everything is split inside of you and you love two people now instead of one.

When you are with the one you love her and the one who is away. When you are with the other you love her and the other who is away. When you are with them both you love them both and the strange part is that you are happy. But as it goes on the new one is not happy then because she can see you love them both although she is still settling for that. When you are alone with her she knows you love her and she believes that if someone loves someone they cannot love anyone else and you never speak about the other to help her and to help yourself although you are past help. You never know and maybe she did not know when she made her decision but sometime in the middle of the winter she began to move steadily and relentlessly toward marriage; never breaking her friendship with you wife, never losing any advantage of position, always preserving an appearance of complete innocence, going away elaborately but only being away at any time long enough so that you would miss her too badly.

The winter of the avalanches was like a happy day in childhood compared to this last winter.

The new and strange girl that now owned half of you, once she had decided to marry, you could not say decided to break up the marriage because that was only a necessary step, a regrettable step, not an end, probably passed over or avoided in thinking, made only one grave mistake. She undervalued the power of remorse.

It was necessary that I leave Schruns and go to New York to straighten out who I was publishing with after the first book of stories. It was a bitter winter on the North Atlantic and there was snow knee deep in New York and when I got back to Paris I should have caught the first train from the Gare de l'Est that would take me down to Austria. But the girl I was in love with was in Paris now, still writing to my wife, and where we went and what we did and the unbelievable wrenching, kicking happiness, selfishness and treachery of everything we did, gave me such happiness and un-killable dreadful happiness so that the black remorse came and hatred of the sin and no contrition, only a terrible remorse.

When I saw my wife again standing by the tracks as the train came in by the piled logs at the station, I wished I had died before I ever loved anyone but her. She was smiling, the sun on her lovely face tanned by the snow and sun, beautifully built, her hair red gold in the sun, grown out all winter awkwardly and beautifully, and Mr. Bumby standing with her, blond and chunky and with winter cheeks looking like a good Vorarlberg boy.

"Oh Tatie," she said, when I was holding her in my arms, "you're back and you made such a wonderful successful trip. I love you and we've missed you so."

I loved her and I loved no one else and we had a lovely magic time while we were alone. I worked well and we made great trips, and it wasn't until we were out of the mountains in late spring, and back in Paris that the other thing started again. Remorse was a fine good thing and with a little luck and if I'd been a better man it might have saved me for something worse probably instead of being my true and constant companion for the next three years.

Maybe the rich were fine and good and the pilot fish was a friend. Certainly the rich never did anything for their own ends. They collected people then as some collect pictures and others breed horses and they only backed me in every ruthless and evil decision that I made and all of the decisions seemed so inevitable and logical and fine and all had been brought about by deceit. It wasn't that the decisions were wrong although they all turned out badly finally from the same fault of character that made them. If you deceive and lie with one person against another you will eventually do it again. If some person is able to do it to you once another person will do it again. I had hated these rich because they had backed me and encouraged me when I was doing wrong. But how could they know it was wrong and had to turn out badly when they had never known all the circumstances? It was not their fault. It was only their fault for comeing into other people's lives. They were bad luck for people but they were worse luck to themselves and they lived to have all of their bad luck finally to the very worst end that all bad lucks could go.

For the girl to deceive her friend was a terrible thing but it was my fault and blindness that this did not repel me. Having become involved in it and being in love I accepted all the blame for it myself and lived with the remorse.

The remorse was never away day or night until my wife had married a much finer man than I ever was or ever could be and I knew that she was happy.

But that winter before I knew that I would ever get back into the badness we had a lovely time at Schruns and I remember all of it and the comeing of that spring in the mountains and how much my wife and I loved and trusted each other truly and how happy we were that all the rich were gone and how I thought we were invulnerable again. But we were not invulnerable and that was the end of the first part of Paris, and Paris was never to be the same again although it was always Paris and you changed as it changed. We never went back to the Vorarlberg and neither did the rich. I do not think even the pilot fish ever went back. He had new places to pilot the rich to and finally he became a rich himself. But he had his bad luck first and it was worse than anyone's.

Nobody climbs on skis now and almost everybody breaks their legs but maybe it is easier in the end to break your legs than to break your heart although they say that everything breaks now and that sometimes, afterwards, many are stronger at the broken places. I do not know about that now but this is how Paris was in the early days when we were very poor and very happy.

are organized everywhere. They even fire canon now and use mortars to start the avalanches.

No one can ever say they will not break a leg now under certain conditions. Breaking a heart is different. Some people say there is no such thing. Certainly you can not break it if you do not have it and many things unite to take it away from those who started with it. Perhaps there is nothing there. *Nada*. You can take this or not. And it can be true or not. There are philosophers who explain it very well.

In writing there are many secrets too. Nothing is ever lost no matter how it seems at the time and what is left out will always show and make the strength of what is left in. Some say that in writing you can never possess anything until you have given it away or, if you are in a hurry, you may have to throw it away. In much later times than these stories of Paris you may not have it ever until you state it in fiction and then you may have to throw it away or it will be stolen again. They say other things too but do not pay them too much attention. They are the secrets that we have that are made by alchemy and much is written about them by people who do not know the secrets or the alchemy. There are many more explainers now than there are good writers. You need much luck in addition to all other things and you do not always have it. This is regrettable but nothing to complain about as you should not complain of those explainers who tell you how you do it and why, if you do not agree with them. Let them explain it all but it must be difficult to reconcile the nothingness you know and the part where you live in other people. Some wish you luck and others do not. Good writing does not destroy easily but you must be careful making jokes.

Then you remember Evan the last time in Cuba when he came over with the pancreas cancer still draining. He was dressing it himself and covering the horses at the Gulfstream

Park for the morning *Telegraph*. He was ahead on his work and he flew over. He had not brought the morphine he needed nor a prescription because they said it was so easy to get in Cuba and it wasn't. There had been a crackdown. He had come to say goodbye. But naturally he would not say it. You could smell the discharge from the cancer draining.

"The doctor will certainly bring it," he said. "There's something holding him up. I'm so sorry about the pain, Hem, and being a nuisance."

"He should be here by now."

"Let's remember all the funny parts about the old days and the great people. Remember Desnos? That was a wonderful book he sent you."

"Remember the time you turned up in Madrid from the hospital at Murcia in *alpargatas* in the snow when you were on convalescent leave after you'd been wounded and you slept under the covers across the foot of the bed and John Tsanakas slept on the floor and John cooked for us?"

"Good John. Remember the wolf when he was a herd boy? I was self conscious about coughing so much. It never means a thing when I cough blood but it's embarrassing. You know Paris was a happy time and Key West was quite wonderful too. But Spain was much the best."

"And the other war. How did you ever get in really?"

"They'll always take you if you really want to go. I took it very seriously and I made master sergeant. It was so easy after Spain. It was rather like being back in school and quite a lot like being with the horses. Combat was interesting as a problem."

"I have all the poems stashed away."

The pain was very bad now and we had remembered so many truly funny things and great people.

"You were very thoughtful about them, Hem. It is not

that things should be published. But I believe now that it is important that they exist. We've both existed quite a lot haven't we Hem? And you wrote awfully well about *Nada*."

"*Nada y pues Nada*," I said. But I remembered the Gulf Stream and the sea and other things.

"You don't mind if I'm serious, Hem. It's been so good to talk about Monsieur Dunning and *le fou dans le cabanon* on that wonderful voyage on the old Paris and the disappearance of Mr. Vosper and André and Jean. The two of them. The waiters. And André Masson and Joan Miro and what happened to them. Remember when you had me on the allowance from the bank and the paintings I bought then? But you must keep on because you write for all of us."

"Who's all of us?"

"Please don't be difficult. I mean us of the early days and the best parts and the bad parts and Spain. Then this other one and everything since and the times now. You have to put in the fun and the other that only we know who have been at some strange places in some strange times. Please do it even when you want to never think about it. And you have to put in now. I am so busy with the horses that I don't know about now. Only my now."

"I'm sorry he's late with that stuff, Evan. That stuff is our now for today."

"It's only pain," he said. "There must be some good reason for the delay."

"We'll go in and find some. Isn't it operable Evan?"

"No. It's been operated of course. Should we not talk about our bodies? I'm so happy your tests are negative. That's wonderful, Hem. You'll forgive me speaking so seriously about your writing. I'm asking you to do the opposite of what I've done about my poetry. You understand why. We never had to make explanations to each other. I write about my now. It is the horses. You have a very interesting now. And you've made me presents of many places and people."

"Let's go in and find some, Evan. I had a whole bit left from the boat. But I did not like to leave it around the place so I burned it probably."

"We might miss him on the way."

"I'll call another doctor. There's no sense waiting longer when it is unbearable."

"Please don't bother. I should have brought it myself. I'm sure he will be coming. I'll just go over to the little house a moment if you don't mind and lie down. Hem, you won't forget about the writing?"

"No," I said. "I won't forget about the writing."

I went out to the telephone. No, I thought. I would not forget about the writing. That was what I was born to do and had done and would do again. Anything they said about them, the novels or the stories or about who wrote them was all right by me.

But there are *remises* or storage places where you may leave or store certain things such as a locker trunk or duffel bag containing personal effects or the unpublished poems of Evan Shipman or marked maps or even weapons there was no time to turn over to the proper authorities and this book contains material from the *remises* of my memory and of my heart. Even if the one has been tampered with and the other does not exist.

FRAGMENTS

The following fragments are transcriptions of handwritten drafts of false starts for the introduction. They are gathered in item 122 in the Hemingway Collection at the John F. Kennedy library in Boston.

This book is fiction. I have left out much and changed and eliminated and I hope Hadley understands. She will see why I hope. She is the heroine and the only person who had a life that turned out well and as it should except certain of the rich.

This book is fiction. I have left out much and changed and eliminated and I hope Hadley understands. A book of fiction may eliminate and distort but it tries to give a fictional picture of a time and the people in it. No one can write true fact in reminiscences; Evan would back you up but he is dead. Scott would disagree. Miss Moorehead would sue if you published anything against Walsh and she had many letters and much basis to sue on. The story about Walsh will have to come out.

This book is all fiction and the fiction may throw some light on what has been written as fact. Hadley is the heroine and I hope she will understand and forgive me writing fiction, some others never will. It is hopeless not to expect to be sued by people all of whose names begin with Miss.

*   *   *

This book is fiction. But there is always a chance that such a work of fiction may throw light on what has been written as fact.

There is much about poverty but it was not all poverty. Hadley would know and understand why certain things were altered I hope and why it was fiction. She would understand why fiction is fiction and when it is fact. Other people will not understand why they are included or not included. Everyone sees it differently and nearly forty years are gone. Characters that seemed strongest and most important to themselves are not there afterwards although, to themselves, they are always more there than anyone. Most of the voyages are not there nor many people that we loved and cared for deeply. It has been cut ruthlessly as fiction should be.

The worst part of it is that you cannot publish it after you are dead because people will still sue even though you change the names and call it fiction as it is. Hadley would not sue because she is the heroine and would understand when you wrote fiction with her in it.

This book is fiction but there is always a chance that such a work of fiction may throw some light on what has been written as fact.

It was necessary to write as fiction rather than as fact and Hadley would understand I hope why it was necessary to use certain materials or fiction rightly or wrongly. All remembrance of things past is fiction and this fiction has been cut ruthlessly and people cut away just as most of the voyages are gone along with people that we cared for deeply. Only they knew certain things. Other people are not there as people are not there in life afterwards although, to themselves, they are always more there than anyone.

There is no last chapter. There were fifty. I hope some people will understand and forgive the fiction and why it was made that way. It has been cut ruthlessly and many things changed. Many voyages have been omitted along with many people. There is no catalogue of omissions or subtractions. The lesson that it teaches has been omitted. You may insert your own lesson and the tragedies, generosities, devotions, and follies of those you knew, unscramble them as in an instrument of transmission and insert your own. You will be wrong of course as I was.

Two things are important. Nothing lasted with us no matter how well intended and they ski much better now than they did in our time. Nobody has to climb on seal skins anymore unless they want to but they are beautifully instructed now and are better in everything. People break their legs and in the world some people still break their hearts. They come down faster and they drop like birds that know many secrets. They have no time to tell their secrets as they pass. Everyone knows many secrets now and everyone has written everything and will write more. It would be fine if it could all be true but lacking that I have attempted in this fiction only to make it interesting. Nobody was invulnerable but we thought we were then and hearing someone's voice over the telephone you know they still are and that they deserve it.

This book is fiction and many things have been changed in fact to try to make it a picture of a true time.

There is no formula to explain why this book is fiction nor will it be effective.

It seemed so easy when it started. Then you found mistakes and errors.

This book is fiction and should be read as such. It may throw some light on other books that have been written as fact. I apologize to Hadley for any mis-representations or mistakes or for any errors. She is the heroine of the stories and I hope she understands. She deserves everything good in life including accurate reporting.

This book is fiction but there is always a chance that such a work of fiction may throw some light on what has been written as fact.

Hadley would understand why it could be necessary to write as fiction rather than as fact and she would see what I have used as the materials for fiction rightly or wrongly. Scott has his own fiction and I wrote about his complicated tragedies, his generosities and his devotions and left them out. Others have written of him and I have tried to help them out. Almost everyone is out along with most of the voyages, the people that we knew and loved and the things they and they alone knew. Only a part of the Paris that we knew is in this book and I will not catalogue what is missing. It is not easy to put in the missing all in fiction and it is all in if you leave it out.

They ski much better now and some break their legs and some break their hearts. The latter is important and unfortunate and some good philosophers explain how you can not break them if they were not there and something happened and they did not exist. The important thing is that they should ski better and they do. They also write better and everything including several wars and all that comes between helped on that along with every good writer from the start. Remembrance of Things Past was fiction too.

> *The following fragment may have been intended as a revision for "The Education of Mr. Bumby. It is Item 186 in the Hemingway Collection at the John F. Kennedy library, Boston.*

In those days it was no disgrace to be crazy, but, on the other hand, you got no credit for it. We, who had been at the war, admired the war crazies since we knew they had been made so by something that was un-bearable. It was unbearable to them because they were made of a finer or more fragile metal or because they were simple and understood too clearly.

> *The following fragments are transcribed from handwritten drafts for the ending of the book. They are item 124 in the Hemingway Collection at the John F. Kennedy library, Boston.*

There was much more to write about poor Scott and his complicated tragedies, his generosities and his devotions and I wrote those and left them out. Other people have written about him and the ones who wrote about him, and did not know him, I tried to help out on the parts about him that I knew, telling them of his great generosities and his kindnesses. But this is about the first part of Paris and certain true aspects of it and Scott did not know the early Paris that we knew and loved and worked in and that always seemed different to me from anything that I have ever read about it. All of that Paris you could never put into a single book and I have tried to write by the old rule that how good a book is should be judged, by the man who writes it, by the excellence of the material that he eliminates. So much that was interesting and instructive is gone and this book is an attempt to distill rather than to amplify. André Masson and Miro are not there as they should be and will be nor Gide teaching me how to punish a cat nor how Evan Shipman and Harold Stearns ran through Evan's fortune when he came of age, but this is straight out of Dostoyevsky. Nor did I mention up in the old Stade Anastasie on the rue Pelleport [nor Ménilmontant] where the fighters worked as waiters and training Larry Gains and all the great fights at the old Cirque d'Hiver and the Cirque de Paris nor many of my best friends, Bill Bird nor Mike Strater nor the Black Forest, nor stories of Ezra and of Eliot and Bel Esprit and the time Ezra left me the jar of opium for Cheever Dunning, nor the truth about Ford. I cut ruthlessly and I hope it makes what is in stronger. I left out when it started with Pauline. That would have been a good way to end this book except that it was a beginning not an ending. Anyway I wrote it and left it out. It is intact and it starts another book. You can only write it in fiction of course. It has the most happiness in it and it is the saddest book I know. But it comes later.

There is never any end to Paris but maybe this will give you some true part of the people and places and the country when Hadley and I believed that we were invulnerable. But we were not invulnerable and that was the end of the first part of Paris. Nobody climbs on skis now and almost everybody breaks their legs and maybe it is easier in the end to break your legs than to break your heart although they say that everything breaks now and that, sometimes, many are stronger at the broken places. I do not know about that now, although I remember who said it. But this is how Paris and other places were in the early days when we were very poor and very happy. There is another book about the parts that are missing and there are always the stories that were lost.

So this is the end of it for now. There was never any end to Paris. But this is the end of the first basic part that always seemed different to me from anything that I had ever read about it.

There is much more to write about Scott and his complicated tragedies, generosities and devotions and I wrote them and left them out. Other people have written them and on the parts I knew I tried to help them. This is about the first part of Paris and Scott did not know the early Paris that we knew and loved and worked in. That Paris you could never put into a single book and I have tried to write by the old rule that how good a book is should be judged by the man who writes it by the excellence of the material that he eliminates. The second part of Paris was wonderful although it started tragically enough. That part, the part with Pauline, I have not eliminated but have saved for the start of another book. It is a start rather than an ending.

It could be a good book because it tells many things that no one knows or can ever know and it has love, remorse, contrition, and unbelievable happiness and final sorrow.

That part, the part with Pauline, I have not eliminated but have saved for the start of another book. It is called The Pilot Fish and The Rich and Other Stories.

There is no mention of Ménilmontant nor of the Stade Anastasie up the steep rue Pelleforte where the boxers of the Anastasie stable served as waiters at the tables set out under the trees and the ring was in the garden, nor of training

Larry Gains, nor of the early days of Paolino, nor the great twenty round fights at the Cirque d'Hiver and the Cirque de Paris nor things that only three of my best friends, Charley Sweeney, Bill Bird or Mike Strater knew. I left out most of the voyages and I left out people that I loved or cared for deeply and other people are not there as people are not there in life, afterwards, although, to themselves, they are always more there than anyone.

If, in your time, you have ever heard four honest people disagree about what happened at a certain place at a certain time, or you have ever torn up and returned orders that you requested when a situation had reached such a point that it seemed necessary to have something in writing, or testified before an inspector general when allegations had been made, presenting new statements by others that replaced your written orders and your verbal orders, you, remembering certain things and how they were to you and who had fought and where, you prefer to write about any time as fiction.

There is never any ending to Paris and the memory of each person who has lived in it differs from that of any other. We always returned to it no matter who we were nor how it was changed nor with what difficulties nor what ease it could be reached. It was always worth it and we received a return for whatever we brought to it.

APPENDIX I

CONCORDANCE OF ITEM NUMBERS FOR THE ADDITIONAL PARIS SKETCHES

All of the following item numbers refer to the cataloging system of the Hemingway Collection at the John F. Kennedy Library, Boston, Massachusetts.

"Birth of A New School," Item 155
"Ezra Pound and His Bel Esprit," Item 161
"On Writing in the First Person," Item 179a
"Secret Pleasures," Item 256
"A Strange Fight Club," Item 185
"The Acrid Smell of Lies," Item 180
"The Education of Mr. Bumby," Item 185a
"Scott and His Parisian Chauffeur," Item 183
"The Pilot Fish and the Rich," Item 123
"*Nada y Pues Nada,*" Item 124a

NOTES

INTRODUCTION

1. Mary Hemingway, "The Making of the Book: A Chronicle and A Memoir," *New York Times Book Review*, May 10, 1964, 26–27; Mary Hemingway, *How It Was* (New York: Alfred A. Knopf, 1976), 440, 444.

2. My mother, Valerie Hemingway, remembers my grandfather telling her, when she was working as his secretary in Paris in the fall of 1959, that he got the idea for the Paris sketches after the plane crashes. See Valerie Hemingway, *Running with the Bulls: My Years with the Hemingways* (New York: Ballantine, 2004), 77. She also helped with the typing of the manuscript of *A Moveable Feast*.

3. For a thorough, scholarly examination of the existing manuscripts from the book, see Jacqueline Tavernier-Courbin, *Ernest Hemingway's* A Moveable Feast: *The Making of Myth* (Boston: Northeastern University Press, 1991). See also Gerry Brenner, *A Comprehensive Companion to Hemingway's* A Moveable Feast: *Annotation to Interpretation,* 2 bks. (Lewiston, NY: The Edwin Mellen Press, 2000), which is the most comprehensive scholarly publication on *A Moveable Feast,* and also contains many comments on the manuscript, arranged according to the published chapters.

4. For a reproduction of the letter, see Brenner, book 1 (supra n. 3), following p. 215.

5. Hemingway Papers, John F. Kennedy Presidential Library & Museum, Item nos. 188–89.

6. Ernest Hemingway, *A Moveable Feast* (New York: Charles Scribner's Sons, 1964), 147.

7. See Seán Hemingway, ed., *Hemingway on War* (New York: Scribner, 2003), especially, xxxi; Michael Reynolds, *Hemingway's First War: The Making of* A Farewell to Arms (Princeton: Princeton University Press, 1976).

8. See Michael Reynolds, *Hemingway: The Paris Years* (New York: W.W. Norton and Co. Limited, 1989), 98, footnote 16.

9. See J. Gerald Kennedy, *Imagining Paris: Exile, Writing, and*

American Identity (New Haven: Yale University Press, 1993), especially 128–37; J. Gerald Kennedy, "Hemingway's Gender Trouble," *American Literature* 63.2 (June 1991), 187–207.

10. See, for example, "My Pal the Gorilla Gargantua," *Ken*, July 28, 1938, reprinted in Seán Hemingway, ed., *Hemingway on Hunting* (Guilford, CT: The Lyons Press, 2001), 187–91.

11. See, for example, Bernard J. Poli, *Ford Madox Ford and the Transatlantic Review* (Syracuse: Syracuse University Press, 1967); Arthur Mizener, *The Saddest Story: A Biography of Ford Madox Ford* (New York: The World Publishing Company, 1971).

12. See George Plimpton, introduction in *A Moveable Feast*, Ernest Hemingway (Norwalk, CT: The Easton Press, 1990), v–xi.

13. On Ernest Hemingway's collection of art, see Colette C. Hemingway, *in his time: Ernest Hemingway's Collection of Paintings and the Artists He Knew* (Naples, FL: Kilimanjaro Press, 2009).

14. In the archives of Charles Scribner's Sons Hemingway Correspondence, Princeton University Libraries. Reproduced in Gerry Brenner, *A Comprehensive Companion to Hemingway's* A Moveable Feast: *Annotation to Interpretation*, Book 1 (Lewiston, NY: The Edwin Mellen Press, 2000), 215.

15. Reynolds, *Hemingway: The Paris Years*, 115.

16. In a letter dated February 6, 1961, to Harry Brague, his editor at Scribner's for the book, Hemingway asked for copies of *The Oxford Book of English Verse* and *The King James Bible* for "titleing." See George Plimpton, introduction in *A Moveable Feast*, vii.

17. For an illuminating discussion of this, see Colette C. Hemingway, *in his time*, 1–10.

18. Hemingway's personal copy of *Ulysses*, a first edition imprint published by Sylvia Beach, can be seen at the Hemingway Room of the J. F. Kennedy library in Boston, Massachusetts. Hemingway was deeply impressed with Joyce as a writer and it is likely that he also saw Joyce's own memoir, *A Portrait of the Artist as a Young Man*, as a significant predecessor to *A Moveable Feast*.

19. A. E. Hotchner, *Papa Hemingway: A Personal Memoir* (New York: Random House, 1966), 57.

20. Matthew Broccoli, ed., *The Short Stories of F. Scott Fitzgerald* (New York: Charles Scribner's Sons, 1989), 631–48.

21. Ernest Hemingway, "Living on $1,000 a Year in Paris," *Toronto Star Weekly*, February 4, 1922, in William White, ed., *Dateline Toronto: The Complete Toronto Star Dispatches, 1920–1924* (New York: Charles Scribner's Sons, 1985), 88–89.